ACHIEVING A COLLEGE DEGREE AND THE AMERICAN DREAM, DEBT-FREE!

HOW TO EARN A COLLEGE EDUCATION WITHOUT THE BURDEN OF STUDENT-LOAN DEBT

CHARLES R. GREEN, M.S. Ed.

WESTBOW
PRESS®
A DIVISION OF THOMAS NELSON
& ZONDERVAN

Copyright © 2020 Charles R. Green, M.S. Ed.

All rights reserved. No part of this book may be used or reproduced by any means, graphic, electronic, or mechanical, including photocopying, recording, taping or by any information storage retrieval system without the written permission of the author except in the case of brief quotations embodied in critical articles and reviews.

The information, ideas, and suggestions in this book are not intended to render professional advice. Before following any suggestions contained in this book, you should consult your personal accountant or other financial advisor. Neither the author nor the publisher shall be liable or responsible for any loss or damage allegedly arising as a consequence of your use or application of any information or suggestions in this book.

WestBow Press books may be ordered through booksellers or by contacting:

WestBow Press
A Division of Thomas Nelson & Zondervan
1663 Liberty Drive
Bloomington, IN 47403
www.westbowpress.com
1 (866) 928-1240

Because of the dynamic nature of the Internet, any web addresses or links contained in this book may have changed since publication and may no longer be valid. The views expressed in this work are solely those of the author and do not necessarily reflect the views of the publisher, and the publisher hereby disclaims any responsibility for them.

Any people depicted in stock imagery provided by Getty Images are models, and such images are being used for illustrative purposes only.
Certain stock imagery © Getty Images.

ISBN: 978-1-9736-8409-1 (sc)
ISBN: 978-1-9736-8408-4 (e)

Library of Congress Control Number: 2020902376

Print information available on the last page.

WestBow Press rev. date: 2/5/2020

My Debt-Free series of books is dedicated to my son, Jeff, and his children, Becca, Regan, and Peyton. I hope that the knowledge and lessons within these pages will guide them as they embark on this great journey of higher education and self-reliance without the financial burden of student debt.

Contents

Preface xi
Introduction xv

- What Is Middle Class? xviii
- Why Is the Middle Class Struggling Today? xix
- Reality Check xxiii

Chapter 1 The Good, the Bad, and the Ugly 1

- The Good 1
- The Bad 2
  - Overall Statistics 3
  - Set Up for Failure 5
  - Legislated Slavery 7
- The Ugly 9
  - Legalized Raping and Robbing of College Graduates and Parents 9
  - Parent PLUS College Loans 10
  - What Is Predatory Lending? 11
  - Beneficiaries of Student Loan Defaults 12
- The Devil's in the Details 14
  - Review 15
  - Call to Action 15

Chapter 2 Parents 17

- Parental Naivete 21
- Status and Ego 22
  - Affordability 24

- ○ Expectations 24
- • An Ounce of Prevention 25
  - ○ Life Is a Business, and You Are Your Business 26
  - ○ Acquire Knowledge and Budget 28
- • Tuition and Fees 30
  - ○ Hidden Agendas 31
- • Credit Cards 101 32
  - ○ Credit Card Strategy 34
  - ○ The Fine Print 36
- • Teachable Moments 37
  - ○ What's the Cost? 37
  - ○ Be a Pragmatist First 38
- • Cosigning 41
- • Plan to Win 44
  - ○ A Master Plan in Action 44
  - ○ Make It a Family Affair 46
  - ○ Discuss Money and Success Topics at the Dinner Table ... 47
  - ○ Commitment 47
- • Modeling and Mentoring for Results 50
  - ○ The Man of La Mancha 50
  - ○ Joshua and Gideon 51
- • Taking Command of Income 53
  - ○ Money and Income 54
  - ○ Parable of the Talents—Matthew 25:14–30 54
  - ○ Rule of Thumb on Income 55
- • Spending and Saving 55
  - ○ Needs versus Wants: Knowing the Difference 57
  - ○ The Friendly Hometown Banker 58
- • Being a Value-Based Consumer 59
  - ○ Buy a Used Car 60

Chapter 3   Investing in Success 63

- • Purchase a Rental Property 63
- • The Law of Mind/Action 65
- • Tithing 66
- • The Law of Attraction 67

- ○ The Importance of Networking.. 67
- ○ How Can I Help?.. 67
- ○ Encourage an Active Role in Student Organizations......... 69
- ○ Follow-Up 70
- ○ Value-Based Foundation... 70
- The Doing Phase 72
  - ○ Apply for All Grants and Scholarships.................................. 72
  - ○ Work for the College, Provide Services, and Barter............74
  - ○ Student Employment... 75
  - ○ Tuition Credits, Discounts, and Reimbursements............ 76
  - ○ The Military Option—a Great Way to Pay for College 77
  - ○ Other Possibilities to Investigate... 79
- Value of Working.. 81
  - ○ Down and Dirty Pays... 81
  - ○ Earning Their Way... 83
  - ○ Using Special Skills 84
  - ○ Food Service Opportunities.. 85
  - ○ Earning and Learning 86
  - ○ Summer Jobs 87
- Entrepreneurial Opportunities... 87
  - ○ Create an Investment Fund 88
  - ○ It's Party Time... 88
  - ○ Business Services 88
  - ○ Lawn Care and Related Services... 89
  - ○ Vending-Machine Routes 89
  - ○ Dormitory Services...90
  - ○ Transportation Needs...90
  - ○ Farm/Ranch Opportunities..90
  - ○ Make a Deal with an Author..90
  - ○ The Internet 91
  - ○ Utilize Computer Skills... 91
  - ○ Become a Self-Promoter... 92
  - ○ Out of Necessity Came a Vision 92
  - ○ Start a Janitorial or House-Cleaning Service....................... 94
  - ○ Bookkeeping for Independent Businesspeople 95
  - ○ Personal Expertise/Talent 95

- The One Great Possibility 97
- Call to Action 101

Chapter 4 Grandparents: The Golden Years 103

- Again, the Ugly 105
- Consequences 106
- Grandparents, Be Aware! 106

Chapter 5 Students: College and Career Success 108

- A Dose of the Truth 109
- Learn Your Lessons 110
- Call to Action 117
  - The Bottom Line 118
  - The How 119
  - The Right Dream 120
  - Stand Up 121
- Student Loans as a Financial Tool 122
- Get Serious about Financing Your Education 124

Chapter 6 Educators 126

- Stepping Up to the Plate 126
- Call to Action 127

Chapter 7 Bankers and Lenders Role 129

- Charley's Code of Conduct for Lenders 130

Chapter 8 Politicians 131

- Teachable Moments 133
- Call to Action 134

Afterword 137
About the Author 139

Preface

Before we begin, let's define exactly what education is. The following definition is from Dictionary.com which I believe is a good operational definition for this book:

> "Education is the act or process of acquiring general knowledge, developing powers of reasoning and judgment, as well as preparing one's intellect and skills for **mature** life. An educated person is someone who perceives accurately, thinks clearly, and acts effectively on self-selected goals."

Based on this definition, it's worth asking, before sending students out for a costly college education, will they graduate financially astute and smarter than when they entered as a freshman, or will they be burdened with student-loan debt, possibly for the rest of their lives, because of not having a foundation of financial literacy?

The following material addresses this question. It is fact-based and includes my own personal observations and viewpoints as a former administrator, business owner, parent, grandparent, and concerned citizen. As you will soon note, fluff, sweet talk, and glossing over the issues affecting your future graduate's and my grandkids' current and future financial well-being have been omitted.

The contents of this book may not be what parents, students, educators, lenders, or politicians want to hear or read regarding the lack of financial education in the home and school systems, leading to a proliferation of student loans that may haunt college graduates for the rest of their lives. If your ultimate goal is to provide a pathway for a debt-free college education followed by a middle-class-plus lifestyle and the American dream, you must understand what it takes to avoid the financial pitfalls. Keep this in mind: our thinking and doing determine outcomes and results in our lives. Is your current way of thinking and doing giving you the outcomes and results desired?

My goal is to provide an informative, in-depth look at the good, the bad, and the ugly of student loans and student debt. I will then help you to make smart choices in funding your student's college education. The hope is that ten years from now, you will be able to look back and realize that your student made smart decisions and endured the sacrifices necessary to lead to the successful career and lifestyle hoped for without regrets or having to say, "If only I had chosen differently."

After spending a great deal of time researching this issue, I've come to the conclusion that financial education has a low priority within our educational system and families. In addition, many of today's parents sending their kids to college are enablers. They accept at face value the spin promoted by our federal government, along with financial and educational institutions, that the only way their little darlings can achieve the American dream is with a college degree.

Out of wishful thinking and political spinning, parents and students blindly believe that a college education guarantees a high-paying job. They are convinced that taking on student loans is a small price to pay. Then, in a state of euphoria, students pursue a degree that will not fulfill their expectations, convinced that whatever choice they make, the government will lead them across the River Jordan into the promised land. The wailing and "O woe is me" begins once they realize they have instead been led into an abyss of debt.

Then, pleading innocence, they contend that they had no idea institutions (federal, private, and public) were profiting off their gullibility, forcing indebted students and parents (if they cosigned the loans) to repay those debts without recourse. One must be cognizant and take responsibility for knowing what one has or has not agreed to; ignorance of the law is no excuse. The American dream of an upper middle class lifestyle and financial security in old age will fade away if we allow ourselves to be led astray by misleading information, false hopes, and unrealistic expectations.

Many students make college and career choices without any sort of in-depth planning. Why? Because parents and educators do not demand that they develop analytical thinking and financial skills, nor do they stress the importance of self-reliance. Perhaps it's because they, too, lack these attributes, or the courage to demand students be financially competent and progress toward self-reliance by the time they get to college. If parents and students choose to avoid these details and blindly sign up for student loans, they may very well wind up in what I call educated poverty, their lifestyle and bank accounts filled only with regrets.

Introduction

This book is directed toward the middle class, whose members have chosen to carry a disproportionate share of the student-loan burden of debt. It may be useful to understand some of the background as to why this is happening, although the lessons discussed apply across the spectrum of those in all income classes who are considering sending their children to college.

This may come as a shock, but nowhere in the Declaration of Independence, Constitution, or Bill of Rights does it say that every student is entitled to a college education. What it does say is every American is entitled to life, liberty, and the pursuit of happiness. There are no guarantees, just the opportunity to pursue a higher-level education, if you so desire, with initiative, motivation, and willingness to achieve through your own efforts.

Were those not the qualities that built this country? That mentality is what will get your children a hands-on degree in self-reliance, skills to deal with life's realities, and a high-paying career. If they don't have these qualities, then perhaps a college education is not in their best interest.

The Statue of Liberty symbolizes hope, opportunity, and freedom to progress toward, and achieve, the American dream. Our country was founded on a set of ideals, including the belief that prosperity and success can be acquired through hard work, persistence, and making intelligent choices. Iowa businessman John T. Adams in 1931 defined the American dream this way: "Life should be better, richer and fuller for everyone, with opportunity for each according to ability or achievement regardless of social class or circumstances of birth."

The idea of the American dream is rooted in the US Declaration of Independence, which proclaims that "all men are created equal" and that they are "endowed by their Creator with certain inalienable rights," including "life, liberty, and the pursuit of happiness." The American dream as it applies to college makes the attainment of higher education a possibility by providing opportunity for prosperity and success through hard work, diligence, and strength of purpose. Yet people seem to believe that achieving a degree should be easy, stress-free, and without cost.

A college education is not guaranteed, nor is it an entitlement. It must be earned. The path to the American dream begins with a healthy dose of brutal honesty coupled with the development of real-life skill sets, hard work, and persistence. Without that combination, no amount of dreaming in the world will take you far.

Let's begin with a little test I came up with to get an idea of your values, degree of commitment, mind-set, and attitude on this issue of money, college, planning, and student loans.

Quiz Time

1. How serious are you about acquiring a debt-free college education for your children?

    A) Somewhat serious
    B) Very serious

2. Given the right coaching and tools, do you believe you could make significant financial progress in helping your children achieve a debt-free college education?

    A) Yes
    B) No

3. Do you believe it is okay to be debt-free, earn significant income, and have substantial savings and investment accounts?

    A) Yes
    B) No

4. How many hours per week are you willing to put into pursuing a debt-free college education for your child?

    A) One hour
    B) Two hours

   C) Three hours
   D) None of the above

5. How much money are you saving every month to assist your son or daughter in pursuing a debt-free college education? (Be honest.)

   A) $0–100
   B) $101–200
   C) $201-plus

6. Do you give back to your community with your time, talents, and contributions?

   A) Yes
   B) No

7. Do you generally make good decisions based on sound information?

   A) Yes
   B) No

8. Are you the type of person who is willing to go the distance in the pursuit of long-term objectives?

   A) Yes
   B) No

9. Are you willing to take greater financial control of your life, knowing it is essential in obtaining a debt-free college education for your children?

   A) Yes
   B) No

    The benefits and rewards of a college degree are available to all who are industrious, willing to sacrifice, and resolved in their tenacity to achieve a high-paying career or a better life. Those who grasp this approach most assuredly will succeed. However, according to Harvard University's Institute of Politics, 65 percent of college graduates today think the American dream is dead—an interesting observation when you note that 70 percent of grads borrowed money to go to college.

    The road to a diploma can be paved with hardships and disappointments for those not motivated, persistent, or self-reliant enough to earn their way based on their own efforts. If these individuals ignore strategic career and financial planning along with application of effort, then what in heaven's name would make them think student loans will lead them to the promised land, the American dream?

Without specific self-reliant traits, they can expect a job paying an average or below-average wage, creating additional stress in their lives as they try paying back excessive loans borrowed to finance a pipe dream without substance. Student loans are not a long-term problem-solver, but they most certainly can be a dream-killer. So what will your goal and strategies be in dealing with the challenges of seeking a college degree?

The first part of this book deals with the good, the bad, and the ugly of student loans and student debt, as well as the background and current state of the program. The latter portions provide insight into how parents and students can overcome the many financial challenges a college education imposes. If you are committed to seeking and pursuing a college degree without taking the loan way out, then pay attention and put into play the information and concepts available here and now.

What Is Middle Class?

According to the Pew Research Center, a middle class income falls in the range of $25,000 to $100,000 a year, with a median income of $56,000. The $75,000 spread accounts for the wide variation in cost of living across the country. Surveys indicate that 86 percent of all wage earners actually make less than $75,000 a year, and 50 percent of those folks took home $28,000 or less. The median for a two-income household is also about $56,000, and those of you who are representative of this income level know how difficult it is for a family of four to live a decent middle class lifestyle.

It is estimated, based on IRS and Social Security returns, that only about 20 percent of all wage earners are in the actual middle class. Of the rest, 7 percent are in the upper middle class or wealthy, and everybody else, 73 percent, are lower middle class or poor.

The goals and desired outcomes of many middle class families include the following:

- have a secure and reliable income with benefits
- keep up with expenses
- have a savings safety net in case of health emergencies or job loss
- pay for children's education
- retire comfortably

The reality is that, although a large number of middle class families own homes and have pensions, many have higher mortgages, greater consumer credit, and more student debt than ever before.

Why Is the Middle Class Struggling Today?

The middle class has been in gradual decline since the 1970s. For the purpose of clarity, I feel it's important to provide a few brief historical highlights and insights into what has happened in the past twenty-five years with the escalating cost of education. This will give you an idea of where we've been, where we are, and where we are headed in the future.

During this period, tuition has risen more than 1,000 percent, far exceeding increases in inflation. This is primarily due to governmental policies regarding subsidized student loans. College students and their parents are struggling to keep pace with rising tuition, and they are being forced (or choose) to borrow in historic proportions.

In 1993, the median cost of a four-year education (tuition, room, board, books, fees, and miscellaneous) was approximately $27,000. Today, twenty-five years later, it is estimated at $81,000—almost a 200 percent increase. Household income in 1993 was $46,300, and in 2017 it was $59,000—a 27 percent increase. That represents a significant difference between college cost and household income. After adjusting for inflation, incomes have actually stagnated. Given rising debt levels and increased cost of goods and services, it is extremely difficult for most families to save and cover a large portion of their children's college cost.

Meanwhile, housing costs have increased more than 1,000 percent since 1970, but middle class income has not kept pace, increasing only 400 percent. The 600 percent difference between income and housing costs is a significant reason why there is a debt crisis plaguing this country. The cost of a home in the 1970s was three times the amount of yearly income of that period, whereas today it is six times the amount of yearly income. Consider the following progression:

- In 1990, the median price of a new home was $123,000.
- In 2000, it had risen to $169,000.
- In 2010, it jumped to $222,000.
- In 2015, the price escalated to $293,000.

Here is another example of how things have changed. In the 1960s and 1970s, a true middle class income, with only the father working, could feed a family of four, pay a home mortgage, and have enough left over for a three-year auto loan on a new car. The average price of that car in the 1970s was just less than $5,000. Like housing, that cost has changed over the years:

- In 1990, the median price of a new car was $16,000.
- In 2000, it was $24,300.
- In 2010, it had risen to $29,000.
- In 2015, it was $33,600.

Auto loans now span five, six, or seven years and average $30,000. A Federal Reserve Bank of New York report indicates that millions of Americans are falling behind, and not just on car payments:"Auto loans in 2018 reached a 19-year high exceeding $1.27 trillion in outstanding debt with an average loan balance over $28,000.00. There are now more subprime auto loan borrowers than ever, thus a larger group of debtors at higher risk of delinquency."

The report continues, "By the end of 2018, more than 7 million Americans are at least 90 days behind on autoloan payments, a continuation of an upward trend in play since 2011. Growing delinquencies among subprime borrowers are responsible for this deteriorating performance, and younger borrowers are struggling most acutely to afford their auto loans."

In addition, the study showed household debt topping out at $13.54

trillion in 2018, which makes it more than 21 percent higher than five years earlier, in 2013. The 2018 breakdown of average household debt individually and as a national total was as follows:

credit cards	$16,000	$747 billion
mortgages	$172,800	$8.4 trillion
auto loans	$ 28,500	$1.3 trillion
student loans	$ 49,000	$1.6 trillion

Since 1985, the cost of a college education has increased almost 1,000 percent. In addition, medical expenses have increased 600 percent and food items 250 percent. Other key factors contributing to the decline of the middle class include government immigration, economic, and tax policies and laws implemented during the last half of the twentieth century.

The greatest growth of the middle class occurred in the mid-twentieth century during a period of low immigration. That began changing in the 1960s when Congress enacted, and President Johnson signed into law, the Immigration and Naturalization Act of 1965. It created one of the greatest upsurges of immigration in the nation's history, and today more than a million immigrants a year are admitted to the United States., not including the millions of illegal aliens crossing the borders. This law ushered in an era of mass immigration and impacted the lives and income of millions, especially the middle class. Other laws and agreements affecting the decline include the following:

- General Agreement on Tariffs and Trade (GATT), updated in 1993
- North American Free Trade Agreement (NAFTA) in 1994
- The World Trade Organization (WTO) in 1995
- H-1B, the Border Security, Economic Opportunity and Immigration Modernization Act, in 1998

H-1B is a temporary visa program allowing American employers to hire foreign professionals with college degrees and "highly specialized knowledge" in science and technology to meet the corporations' needs for particular skills. Multinational companies have obtained thousands of temporary visas to bring in foreign workers who have taken over jobs once held by Americans.

These economic policies also gave American corporations government-granted tax advantages to begin offshoring and outsourcing American jobs, manufacturing, and businesses to Mexico, China, and other nations—with no obligation to pay these foreign workers prevailing or market wages. The government's and corporations' actions were for the sole purpose of moving production out of this country in order to obtain manufactured goods at a lower cost under the guise of enhancing shareholder value and being part of the "global economy."

The US Department of Commerce claimed that "US multinational corporations, the big brand-name companies that employ a fifth of all American workers ... cut their work forces in the US by 2.9 million during the 2000s while increasing employment overseas by 2.4 million." Obviously, 500,000 workers were left stranded in unemployment lines as high-paying union jobs in the auto, building, and appliance industries, as well as retail manufacturing, were moved out of the United States. Those losses, combined with inflation, began wiping out any middle class wage gains.

During this period, productivity and corporate profits substantially increased, along with CEO pay, which has risen more than 1,000 percent since the 1950s. Meanwhile, middle class income decreased by 5 percent, while total wealth dropped 28 percent. This income decline and disparity has significantly contributed to the high levels of debt being carried today. Bankruptcy law changes also came into play, exempting student loan borrowers from bankruptcy protection. Corporate borrowers, of course, still retained their protection, with an effective way out should financial hard times occur.

Protective bankruptcy laws in place prior to 1990 kept excessive lending, borrowing, and costs in check. Once the government decreed that every child should have a college degree, legislation was enacted giving lenders guarantees that they could not lose in their lending practices and would profit from issuing student loans to any and all students wanting to go to college. Those lender guarantees and the bankruptcy laws working in their favor have been a financial boon for lenders, the federal government, and educational institutions. This had the unintended or intended consequence of a massive rise in the cost of attending college.

As the cost of college increased, more people were saddled with tens of thousands of dollars in student loans. Under ever-increasing pressure to maintain their place in the middle class, many Americans turned to borrowing on credit cards and against the equity in their homes. Indebtedness has grown, and savings have evaporated, forcing people to dig deeper into their equity, including pensions, and take on additional part-time work to make ends meet.

Reality Check

Needless to say, the financial challenges in obtaining a college education in a high-paying field have never been greater. Today, students who aspire to a future upper middle class lifestyle need to pursue careers in science, technology, engineering, and math—the so-called STEM fields that earn a premium in pay. It is my hope that you will keep this background information in perspective and use it to plan your course of action to help you and your student reach your goals of a rewarding and beneficial outcome without burdening and overwhelming your family's future with excruciating debt.

Now let's get to the meat and potatoes of this book and see if there are some golden nuggets to help you navigate, overcome, and prosper from these challenges. We'll start with a personal reality check to determine your mind-set as it pertains to money management. When we look within ourselves for answers, many times we're forced to face some truths about who we are, where we're at, and where we're going in life. The beauty of looking within provides an opportunity for personal growth.

The following is a self-reflection quiz, and your answers may reveal your ability to teach kids the facts about money. Be honest with yourself. I've made it easy, with most questions requiring only a yes or no answer. Your answers have long-range implications for your and your children's future, so don't hesitate to expand your *no* answers into a specific plan for improvement.

Quiz Time

1. Am I a good role model for my children regarding the use of credit cards, loans, budgeting, and financial planning?

   A) Yes
   B) No

2. Am I willing to share with and teach my child the realities of cash and debt management?

   A) Yes
   B) No

3. Am I comfortable talking with my children about money?

   A) Yes
   B) No

4. Do I involve my kids when paying household bills so they understand the process of bill paying in relation to earned income?

   A) Yes
   B) No

5. Do I share the money mistakes made and the lessons learned from those mistakes?

   A) Yes
   B) No

6. Do I teach them responsibility and accountability in the use of money and credit?

   A) Yes
   B) No

7. Do I talk, practice, and advocate financial self-reliance and financial competency to my children?

   A) Yes
   B) No

8. Do my children feel a sense of entitlement? Do they expect to have whatever they want, when they want it?

   A) Yes
   B) No

9. Do my kids understand the value of money?

   A) Yes
   B) No

How did you score on these questions? Did you earn a passing grade of at least eight yeses? Which specific questions need the most work in order for you to obtain and model a degree in family financial success? Remember, the desire and motivation to pursue and achieve financial freedom must be modeled in the home.

If you need some reinforcement on the importance of this topic, I encourage you to talk to students who've graduated with student loans and credit card debt to see how it has affected their standard of living and their ability to buy a newer car and/or home. Ask them if they had it to do over again, would they have done it differently? Let their answers be your guide.

Chapter 1
The Good, the Bad, and the Ugly

The Good

Student loans are only one tool to finance the education of a marketable, in-demand future college graduate. These loans must be used shrewdly, judiciously, and with caution. Borrowing must be for the express purpose of preparing for a career yielding not only a high middle class income but also a future of opportunity and prosperity without the burden of debilitating debt.

Unfortunately, the majority of student borrowers, their parents, and their cosigners fail to develop or adhere to a specific financial plan to achieve the desired result: a college degree that will generate a reasonable return on investment. In too many cases, borrowers and cosigners are afflicted with a case of avoidance syndrome, which keeps them from grasping, embracing, and understanding the true cost and potential long-term consequences of relying on loans for things like housing, food, entertainment, and in too many cases, spring break. These are areas student loans were not designed to cover. Failure to invest personal funds, make work commitments, and save money can land these students and their families in educated poverty.

Loans serve a purpose when used properly for the right reasons. A student loan, with its long-term repayment implications, should only be considered as a last resort or in an emergency when all other possibilities have been exhausted.

The Bad

Student loans will not guarantee the American dream; in fact, they may guarantee the loss of it. Will your college graduate, former student, or constituent be left wondering, "If I'm so smart, gifted, and educated, then why am I so broke?" CEO of U, Inc. Lirel Holt describes the problem this way:

A form of enslavement has descended upon us and as ridiculous as it seems, we have allowed and encouraged it to take over our lives. It is *economic slavery!* Swiftly and quietly, without noticeable fanfare, it has become rampant in the United States with many people *deliberately* pulling the yoke of that burden over their heads and placing it firmly upon their shoulders! *It's crazy!*

Why is this happening? This crisis has been developing throughout our entire social and economic structure and began accelerating when Congress gave lenders protection but kept borrowers at risk. The lenders and politicians were prepared, but there was no effort to prepare student borrowers or their parents for what was to come.

Financial education begins in the home and should continue to be a key factor in our educational system, which professes to prepare students for life after school. However, what is professed is not always reality. Financial education in the United States is an iffy proposition. According to Wallet Literacy Survey, fewer than 50 percent of states require a personal finance class in high school. That's right: the majority of students in the United States are not required to learn personal financial and management concepts and skills.

Fewer than 17 percent of US students are required to take any personal finance course to graduate high school. People in middle class and low-income households are the major victims of this neglect, and their debt levels show it. A higher priority placed on achieving financial literacy in all grade levels through a better, required financial education model could definitely have an impact on these figures. However, the driving force behind this must come from the home, be embraced by our school systems, and be supported by our politicians.

Alan Greenspan, former chairman of the Federal Reserve Board, has made this suggestion: "In many respects, improving financial education at the elementary and secondary school level is essential to providing a foundation for financial literacy that can help prevent younger people from making poor financial decisions that can take years to overcome." If you want your children to live the American dream, you must be the driving force behind their achieving financial literacy.

Overall Statistics

I'm sharing the following information to alert you to the hazards, obstacles, and cavernous money pits lying in wait if you take on student loans as a way to finance a college education. The goal is to spur you into action to avoid the burden of excessive student loans, unnecessary credit card debt, and economic servitude. This should be of critical importance to all parents, students, educators, and politicians who believe in the American dream.

Before signing on the dotted line, you must know what the liability, hardships, and consequences to the borrower (student) and/or cosigner (parent) could be in the event circumstances lead to defaulting on these loans. Why is this important? Before delving into the details, it is best to give you an overall snapshot of the current student loan debt situation. Here are a few statistics from the Federal Reserve Bank of New York Consumer Credit Panel/Equifax Federal Student Loan Portfolio that will give you a better idea of where the nation stands with its second leading form of debt:

According to the U.S. Department of Education, he national student loan debt approaches $1.6 trillion. This is $600 billion higher than credit card debt. It continues to grow because most student borrowers and their parents have little understanding of how the loan program works. Consequently, it has become the largest financial asset on the federal government's balance sheet, representing almost 52 percent of total assets, another consequence from a lack of financial literacy in the home and schools.

The number of student loan borrowers is 46 million, or 70 percent of college students. This number of borrowers is larger than the populations of Canada, Poland, North Korea, and Australia, and four times greater than the population of Sweden. Another interesting point, according to

Standard & Poor's Global Financial Literacy Survey, is that the United States ranks fourteenth in literacy behind such countries as Denmark, Canada, Germany, the United Kingdom, Australia, and New Zealand. And by the way, credit card use and student debt in America are among the highest in the world, which may stem from the low priority given to financial education by our leaders.

The student loan default rate continues to rise. In 2016, it was 12 percent in 2019, it has increased to about 25 percent, or 11 million student borrowers who are in default on the books. Even in default, interest, fees, and penalties keep adding on. The student loan delinquency rate is 5.41 percent, and the average debt per student borrower is $28,000. Other points to consider:

- The class of 2018 has the distinction of being the most indebted graduating class ever, amassing a debt of more than $75 billion, which exceeds the total student loan debt of 1980 by $21 billion.
- 70 percent of college graduates have an average student debt of $39,000, not including fees and compounding interest, with payments exceeding $400 per month—and the majority also have accumulated credit card debt of $3,000–4,000.
- The average college senior graduated with a debt burden (student loans and credit cards) of more than $40,000 (a conservative estimate; in reality, it may be closer to $70,000). Now these workers can expect to retire when they reach seventy-two years of age.

Another point relates to postgraduates: 40 percent of the overall student loan debt total is accounted for by graduate borrowers ($563 billion). Many put their undergraduate loans in deferment during this period, not realizing or acknowledging the additional fees and continued accumulation of interest on interest plus added fees and new loan amounts borrowed for their graduate program.

In too many cases, those seeking postgraduate degrees use much of their loan money for living expenses, thereby ballooning the amount of student debt that must be repaid when they leave school. The total amount easily exceeds $75,000, and for medical professionals—such as doctors, chiropractors, dentists, and veterinarians—the amount may easily exceed $200,000. Let's not forget the legal profession, as a great many of those graduates owe well over $100,000.

In most cases, the need to pay off these loans creates considerable financial difficulty, especially when graduates discover that high-paying jobs do not exist in their degree fields. The cost of living may also be more expensive than planned as they begin new careers. A majority of students have not been taught financial skills, either in the home or within our educational system. A possible outcome is that many students will allow their parents to go broke supporting them.

Too many parents have allowed themselves, with the influence and support of the federal government, educational system, and financial institutions, to commit a grievous disservice to their young adults. Failing to stress financial education and critical thinking throughout the early years of childhood development and education sets you and your children up to become victims of the system by falling into a poverty, entitlement, and/or debt mentality.

A special few of those parents and educators who read this will embrace these facts, heed the warnings, and look for alternatives to help their students pursue a debt-free college education. Those who don't are compromising young adults' long-term future by allowing them to take the easy, burdensome, loan way out in the pursuit of a higher education. Don't be one of those.

Set Up for Failure

Many folks have bought into the government's economic mantra, which is this: the secret to our success is borrowing, spending, and debt accumulation. Congress continues to follow the path of accumulating debt through borrowing and spending. The term *fiscal responsibility* is loosely used and rarely practiced. Financial literacy might have been a shortcoming in Congress's education as well.

And how has that worked for them and us? Let's see—we have a national debt rapidly approaching $21 trillion; 23 million Americans are unemployed or underemployed; and some workers have left the workforce entirely. Included in this number, the Associated Press reports, are 54 percent, or 945,000, of recent college grads out of a total of 1,750,000 who either have no job or are underemployed. They have landed jobs in areas such as bartending and pizza delivery. Is this what they consider success?

Let's look at where this philosophy has taken us. Americans have followed Congress and the administration's lead by taking on more than $14 trillion in debt, including $1 trillion in credit card debt, $1.5 trillion in student loan debt, $9 trillion in mortgages, more than $1 trillion in car loans, and Lord knows what else. This adds up to a combined debt of almost $47.5 trillion—not including bailouts. How can America pay off national as well as personal debt when more than 20 million people are in assorted states of job distress and 47 percent of our current population is enrolled in various welfare programs and pay no taxes?

A government economist tells us, "The US economy will recover as consumer borrowing and spending increases. The ability of our citizens to borrow money is seen as an important step for economic growth." Has taking on credit card and student loan debt created economic growth and prosperity in your household? Wait a minute, does this mean we must seek and attain better-paying jobs in order to borrow, spend, and pay more taxes? To secure those better-paying jobs, are they telling us it's imperative our young adults and displaced workers pursue college educations and incur vast amounts of debt in order to achieve the American dream?

Remember, 70 percent of college graduates have accumulated in excess of $35,000 (in too many cases, it's over $75,000) in student loan and credit card debt, not including the compounding effect of interest upon interest. The wake-up call begins when graduates cross the stage, pick up that diploma, and are served notice that student loans are due and payment must begin immediately. That's when reality hits them in the seat of the pants. They discover that high-paying jobs in their degree field are not sufficient to support debt repayments and cost of living. With that comes the realization that they have allowed themselves to be led like sheep down the path toward economic servitude. They have earned their degrees in avoidance and gullibility.

Most students underestimate the impact of interest and fees on loans while overestimating their earning power to pay loans off after graduation. By miscalculating these factors—especially earning power—many graduates find their beginning salaries are $10,000 to $15,000 less per year than expected, and their loan payments are in excess of $500 per month. Most of that $500 goes toward interest alone. Thus, the principle remains at or near the original loan amount and cycle continues. Set another plate at the table, Mom and Dad. Your grad is coming home!

Adding to the burden and stress, joblessness among adults ages twenty to twenty-four remains stalled at 12.5 percent, and over half of all student loans are now delinquent or in deferral. Additionally, more than 13 percent of graduates are defaulting on their loans within three years of leaving college. Is there a correlation between the unemployment rate of 12.5 percent and the 13 percent of graduates defaulting on their loans?

The following personal confession is but one of many:

> I wish someone would have talked to me about this before I borrowed. My situation was a bit different, as my folks weren't a part of my college career ever. I borrowed from the government every year and thought it great fun to take more than needed. I'm twenty-six years old and owe $70,000 in student loans. Now my repayment (beginning after deferment is no longer an option) will take me at least thirty years to pay off. It's frightful, and I wish someone would have told me that when I was eighteen!

Unfortunately, this is an all-too common scenario among today's college graduates. To hear more about these kinds of self-inflicted burdens, read the newspapers, listen to the morning and evening news, or go on the internet. Such stories are plentiful and indicative of the consequences of student loans and irrational decisions. I think you understand why this graduate wishes to remain anonymous.

Legislated Slavery

Federal and private guaranteed student loans are the exception among loan instruments in the nation's history. Student loans are treated differently than other consumer loans, where the borrower has the option of bankruptcy and default protection. All other federal loan guarantee programs in the United States, secured or unsecured, provide bankruptcy protection should circumstances dictate. Farm loans, FEMA loans, SBA loans, DOE 1705, and all other government loans and guarantees—not a single one, with the exception of student loans, is exempted from bankruptcy discharge.

Additionally, certain segments of the economy—such as airlines and the automotive, energy, and financial industries—get the full benefit and protection of bankruptcy laws. The others—consumer and student borrowers—do not. You are required to pay your loans back no matter what the circumstances. Debts from gambling and other consumer debts can be erased via bankruptcy, but not education debt. It is nearly impossible to file for bankruptcy. These debts continue to grow when a borrower is unable to pay, and they can even follow a borrower to the grave.

The student loan lending program has become the worst big-government predatory-lending system this country has ever seen. The federal government profits well over $50 billion per year and even profits off of defaults. Additionally, profits from this program are being used to fund other government programs. Let's not misunderstand or forget this. Removing bankruptcy protection from student loans only benefits the lenders. Sallie Mae officials have listed preserving the inability to discharge education debt in bankruptcy as their second most important goal. Exactly why is that?

While no one ever wants to file for bankruptcy, bankruptcy protection can and does afford citizens who have incurred insurmountable debt a legal process for resolving those debts, allowing them to continue on to productive lives. It is a critically important freedom to have, serving as a protection against abuses that frequently occurred for debtors. Until 1976, you could discharge any student loan along with other government loans in bankruptcy. However, when the 1978 Bankruptcy Reform Act was passed by Congress, it included a seven-year repayment condition on the discharge of student loans in bankruptcy, meaning the loan had to become due at least seven years prior to filing.

That was the beginning of taking away any and all relief for those who had taken on student loans to finance their college education. This law was followed by the 1998 amendments to the Higher Education Act, which included the following:

- Bankruptcy protection was removed completely for the vast majority of borrowers.

- Statutes of limitations for the collection of student loan debt were removed.
- Student loans were exempted from state usury laws.
- Student loans were specifically exempted from coverage under truth-in-lending laws and the Fair Debt Collection Practices Act.

Higher education state guaranty agencies were exempted from the Fair Debt Collection and Practices Act; however, for-profit student loan collection companies were required to adhere.

In 2005, the Bankruptcy Abuse Prevention and Consumer Protection Act was signed into law, including a provision making it nearly impossible to discharge private student loans in bankruptcy. This legislation, with its ever-increasing regulations, came about as a result of intense lobbying by financial institutions seeking loan guarantees from the federal government. Now those lenders can grant loans to high-risk borrowers and not have to suffer financial consequences should the debtor default. The interest rates on these loans rival those of mafia loan sharks. Which leads us to …

The Ugly

Justifications for these acts and regulations were not supported with substantiated facts. The enactment of these laws were based solely on the so-called credibility and financial enhancements various lending institutions used to persuade the all-seeing, all-benevolent Washington fathers to do their will. President Carter built the coffin with the passing of the Bankruptcy Reform Act of 1978. President Clinton put the lid on it with the passing of the 1998 amendments to the Higher Education Act. President Bush nailed the coffin shut with the passing of the 2005 Bankruptcy Abuse Prevention and Consumer Protection Act.

Legalized Raping and Robbing of College Graduates and Parents

What is unbelievable is that this legislation gave the guarantors of the loans the right to add a 25 percent increase to the balance of loans immediately upon default, which could happen even if the borrower missed one or two payments. Plus, this legislation provided for annual collection rates to be attached to the debt. If you defaulted on a loan, you were subject not only to a large increases in debt, you also faced annual collection rates of up to 25 percent of the balance of the loan.

Factor in the compounding effect of these added penalties and fees, all of which can take that initial outstanding loan balance of $50,000 to a whole different level of challenge. In this case, a new outstanding principal balance can escalate to $150,000 in a relatively short period—and follow the borrower to the grave. In addition to these added penalties and fees, congress granted the industry unbelievable methods for recovery of the increased debt. This included the power of wage, Social Security, and disability garnishment; tax seizure; suspension of state-issued professional licenses; and even termination from public employment.

According to figures provided by the US Department of Education, more than 7 million Americans over age fifty now account for $290 billion in debt on federal education loans. Of college students, 69 percent took out student loans. They graduated with an average debt of $29,800, including both private and federal.

Parent PLUS College Loans

This is an overview of a lending program gone amuck in the student loan arena. It's called Parent PLUS and specifically targets parents—allowing them to borrow, without limit, $10,000 to $200,000 or more plus origination fee. Funds from these loans can be used to cover any and all college expenses for their children not covered by scholarships or grants. All that is needed to qualify is a credit score over 600. Income, current or future, is given little consideration in the application process. The amount borrowed may be unrelated to parents' ability to pay it back

How's that working out? At the end of 2017, approximately 3.5 million parents borrowed about $84.0 billion in Parent PLUS loans from the federal government. Today, default rates are approaching 8 percent and climbing. Consider the class of 2018: 14 percent of parents took out an average of $35,600 in federal Parent PLUS loans. More than 10 percent of those loans are ninety days delinquent, and almost 25 percent are in default (360 days past due). Factor in the possibility of wage, Social Security, or disability garnishment, and the consequences of defaulting on Parent

PLUS loans are the same as defaulting on federal student loans. Penalties can include wage garnishment; seizure of 15 per cent of Social Security and disability benefits; loss of federal and state income tax refunds; usurious collection fees; loss of other assets, including one's estate; and exemption from bankruptcy protection. Now you have a setup for major stress issues leading to unintended consequences.

If parents borrow in excess and students are not willing to do their part to contribute financially, a parent's future income may never be high enough to pay the loan off. Remember, when the payments are due, only the parents are on the hook and liable for the debt. In the event of hardship, payback can be extended from the normal term of ten years to twenty-five years, and all too often into retirement.

These loans represent government lending practices at their worst, and the program has a predatory aspect. Parents encouraged to base their decisions on emotion will easily fall prey and very possibly face financial hardships in the ensuing years. As the program spirals out of control unchecked, hardships increase, and taxpayers' exposure along with college tuition will continue to rise.

It is difficult to believe there was ever a good reason, other than the salesmanship of the lender and gullibility or greed of the government, to lend to parents. There are so many opportunities today to achieve a relatively debt-free college education. However, it does take creativity, industriousness, and sacrifice. This is a burden many will carry from graduation to retirement. Unfortunately, some will commit suicide, others will become homeless, and many will live with the debt for the remainder of their lives.

The conditions imposed on borrowers and cosigners by lenders and allowed by the federal government appear to border on discriminatory and predatory lending practices. Again, these interest rates and practices put Mafia loan sharks to shame.

What Is Predatory Lending?

Predatory lending refers to any lending practice that imposes unfair or abusive loan terms on a borrower, as well as any practice that convinces a borrower to accept unfair terms through deceptive, coercive, exploitative, or unscrupulous actions for a loan that a borrower doesn't need, doesn't want, or can't afford. It's the practice of a lender deceptively convincing borrowers to agree to unfair and abusive loan terms, or systematically violating those terms in ways that make it difficult for the borrower to defend against.

The term may also refer to payday loans and various forms of consumer debt where the interest rates are unreasonably high. Although predatory lenders usually target the less educated, the poor, racial minorities, and the elderly, victims are represented at all income levels, particularly in cases where an unsophisticated borrower is involved.

A very important point to keep in mind is that all of the remedies granted the lenders also apply to the cosigner of the loan in case the original borrower defaults. Many parents think and hope they are doing the right thing (out of guilt or fear) when they cosign for educational loans. They fail to understand (or they simply ignore) possible long-range consequences that may affect their own financial situation.

Although parents believe their child would never default, neither parents nor young adults can know with certainty what their own financial or health situation may be in five, ten, or even fifteen years. You may be approaching retirement age, not planning on additional debt or working beyond retirement. Any substantial change in your health may drastically affect income and your ability to pay off loans.

If you are sixty years of age and older, headed toward retirement, you may find yourself part of the group responsible for more than $43 billion in student loans. If you ignore this with the possible horrendous consequences lying in wait, you are a candidate for Uncle Charley's Cosigner's Anonymous support group. I will explore the pitfalls of cosigning a student loan in more depth later in the book.

Beneficiaries of Student Loan Defaults

In the mid-1970s, Congress began removing long-standing consumer protections from student loans as a result of the intensive lobbying efforts of lending institutions like Sallie Mae, USA Funds, and Consumer Bankers Association. It enacted legislation that made student loans risk-free for the lender thanks to government guarantees. This gave the lenders the freedom to set up defensive, profitable strategies that took full advantage of the situation when borrowers attempted to default.

In the 1998 amendments to the Higher Education Act, Congress passed legislation, again as the result of intense lobbying by the student loan industry, to make delinquent student loan debt extremely profitable for the lender. Now lenders could charge/assess additional penalties and fees along with increased interest rates. This strategy, with the knowledge and backing of the federal government, has generated extremely healthy profits from loan payments, late fees, and default penalties for these lenders.

Here's an interesting bit of information: certain proponents of these tactics try to convince us that these laws and strategies are necessary because student borrowers who default are robbing taxpayers. The truth is, these guarantors and collection companies make a tremendous amount of profit from the collection of these loans. In addition, the federal government also benefits, receiving $1.20 for every dollar paid out in default claims. These laws and regulations have created a huge cash cow or profit center for the federal government, private lenders, and institutions of higher education.

How big a cash cow? The government earned about $66 billion in profits from student loans between 2007 and 2012, or $13 billion per year. It is estimated to be pocketing an additional $185 billion on new student loans made over the next ten years. This raises the question: should the government be in the business of legalized profiteering under the guise of promoting student loans as the affordable way to achieve the American dream?

A key factor to bear in mind is that most educational institutions promoting and originating loans receive fees and incentives from lenders just as they do from companies promoting credit cards on campus. These fees have become profit centers for many of our institutions of higher learning. To them, it's strictly business, and you, the customer, are only a number contributing to the bottom line. Therefore, you must conduct your own financial affairs in like manner: as a business. Be mindful that the best interest of the college or university is not always the best interest of the students.

Our Washington fathers felt the silver lining their pockets. They proceeded to enact laws, rules, and regulations condemning past, current, and future student loan borrowers to a lifetime of challenging debt without a lifeline or support.

The Devil's in the Details

If you have read everything so far, you have acquired sufficient background on the key negative issues regarding student loans that are seldom discussed or disclosed. That leads us into an exploration of the student loan fallacy and its impact on many graduates and their families when they ignore certain basic truths associated with these loans. The whole point of this book is to create a heightened sense of awareness and reinforce positive attitudes and actions needed to achieve a debt-free degree.

You may find some of the commentary too direct and feel that it hits too close to home. You may become angry and wish you could fling this into the recycle bin. Pay attention to those feelings and responses. They may just cause you to alter the course of your thinking and approach to a college education. My goal is to force you to look closely—with a jaundiced, skeptical eye—at your own personal actions and attitudes when it comes to money, college, and student loans.

The true cost of student loans must be taken into account. The last thing you need is to face financial hardships caused by poor, uninformed, and uncourageous decisions. If you want the American dream, you must wake up, put into play strategies necessary to achieve it, and always remember that our thinking and doing determine the outcomes and results in our lives. One of those key strategies is dealing with the affliction known as *avoidance*.

Avoidance is most often thought of as a character flaw possessed by individuals who sidestep tough issues like career decisions, personal problems, obligations, and commitments. However, in this presentation, it can mean rejecting those decisions and actions that might cause one to fall into educated poverty. In this case, avoidance can be a good thing, especially if your goal is to make the right choices and do the right things in pursuit of the American dream.

Review

To help you avoid those pitfalls, let's review what you've learned in this chapter. A student loan (government or private) is a source of financing available to assist college students seeking a higher education. It must be used wisely, with discretion, planning, and understanding of the obligations and commitment required when repayment time rolls around. Unconstrained borrowing can and will lead to the accumulation of a substantial and unmanageable amount of debt, especially when there is not a sustainable or sufficient income available to service the debt and other living costs and demands.

When the borrower fails to make required payments, the loan goes into default without recourse. There might be a slim, outside chance of relief because of hardship available to the borrower and/or cosigner, but don't count on it. At this point, the lender begins adding collection fees, interest rate increases, and other penalties, significantly increasing the loan amount due over and above the original principal borrowed.

Factor in the possibility of wage, social security, or disability garnishment, and you have a setup for major stress issues that can lead to a number of unintended consequences. This is a burden many will carry from graduation to retirement. Unfortunately, some will join the ranks of the homeless, and others will commit suicide.

Call to Action

If a student loan borrower is buried in debt, it appears at this time that the only legal way out is to bring political pressure to bear to get specific bankruptcy laws changed that affect student loan borrowers. These discriminatory laws and regulations should be repealed and/or declared unconstitutional; however, they cannot be changed overnight. If you have read up to this point, then apparently this is an issue of great and personal concern for you. I would highly suggest taking the following actions:

- Contact your congressional and senatorial representatives. Ask them to work on your behalf to rescind or repeal those bankruptcy

laws and regulations that discriminate unfairly against student borrowers.
- Contact legal representatives to file suit against the federal government declaring that the Bankruptcy Reform Act of 1978, the 1998 amendments to the Higher Education Act, and the 2005 Bankruptcy Abuse Prevention and Consumer Protection Act unjustly, discriminately, and prejudicially single out and remove bankruptcy and default protections from student loan borrowers.
- Organize college students, graduates, and parents to bring political pressure to bear by insisting that equal treatment must be applied to borrowers of student and consumer loans.
- Enroll in organizations and business groups that support changes in student loan programs—changes that will bring justice, equality, and fairness for college borrowers.

Chapter 2
Parents

The following are the top ten excuses parents give for not insisting on financial education for their children—and the harsh realities:

1. "Our children have such busy schedules that it's tough to find time to incorporate money matters and effective financial practices into their lives."

   Reality: Parents intentionally avoid teaching and training their children in basic money skills as subconsciously, they feel they have failed to manage their own financial affairs.

2. "My child's only fourteen. She doesn't need to know about money at that age."

   Reality: Mind-set and values regarding money are already ingrained into children by the time they reach eighteen years of age. Unfortunately, if financial education has been avoided during the formative years, social media very possibly becomes their go-to interest over money matters. Financial literacy needs to be learned, embedded, and embraced beginning in the elementary grades and continued through high school so students are prepared to handle their own financial matters responsibly. The obvious advantage is that students will make better career choices so that opportunity will be knocking on their doors at graduation instead of lenders.

3. "Saving and investing are really a hassle, as the small return won't meet our needs or expectations."

   Reality: Parents would rather spend income on high-end consumption items to create the impression of overall prosperity and affluence than save and invest.

4. "I don't have time to work on a budget or plan; we're just trying to make it through the day." (This is the same reason those in the low-income bracket give. They aren't worried about tomorrow; they're worried about the grocery money today.)

   Reality: The average American spends $1.20 for every $1.00 earned because of a lack of disciplined planning for future financial freedom. The concern is for today, wishfully thinking tomorrow will take care of itself. Time is not the key factor in planning; it's the discipline to make it so. Financial freedom and budgeting do go together.

5. "Giving my child a credit card in high school will teach financial responsibility."

   Reality: In fact, this teaches financial *irresponsibility*. Having a credit card won't make children any wiser or richer. When it comes to credit cards, most people, especially teens, don't understand that some company giving them a credit card has absolutely nothing to do with their ability to afford it.

6. "Our children will do as we say because they trust and respect us."

   Reality: Kids learn the most about money from their parents, as they imitate adult actions and watch what parents do even more than listening to what they say. If parents' words don't match their actions, what makes them think their children are going to listen to what they say? Children will copy into their lives the parental model that's put in front of them every day in the home. In today's world, too many parents no longer just raise children;

they protect children, and consequently develop dependent instead of independent young people. This protectionist culture creates a bubble effect around the child, and sometime in the future the bubble will collapse when the reality of life meets the unprepared.

7. "I have nothing saved for me, as I'm using all my extra money for my kids' education, which is my top financial priority."

   Reality: When parents reach retirement, their fixed income and savings may not be enough to cover their own living expenses. Additionally, there may be aging parents to assist. Many will have to downsize their retirement dreams to help their children pay for college. The money parents use for student loan repayment will reduce their ability to pay for other things they want to do in retirement.

8. "I can't say no to my children."

   Reality: Many parents who are financially strapped will still go to great lengths to indulge their children. Self-worth factors are at play when parents choose this behavioral pattern. If the proper foundation through education, discipline, and occasionally tough love hasn't been established, kids will allow their parents to go broke supporting their lifestyle. You can bet these kids will say no or avoid their parents if the roles are reversed.

9. "That's what I'm here for—to make sure my children get a college education."

   Reality: These parents will sacrifice their own financial security for the sake of their children. Today's children live in an age of entitlement and don't always appreciate what they have unless they've learned to earn and save.

10. "Kids shouldn't work while attending college. They need time to be with friends and enjoy the college experience."

   Reality: Kids have never had a problem finding time to socialize. If you pay for everything, where's the motivation for them to learn to become self-sufficient? Are you considering allowing your future graduates, without accountability, to go through college on your dime and on student loans just so they can have freedom to enjoy the college experience without paying a major part of their expenses through earnings, savings, and sacrifice?

Quiz Time

Let's take a short test to check out some of your personal insights about college, debt, and mind-sets. Your answers will be an indicator of personal awareness and whether these issues are important to you.

1. The use of student loans to pay for a college education is smart planning.

   A) True
   B) False

2. Student loans should only be considered when all other possibilities have been exhausted.

   A) True
   B) False

3. Of today's undergraduates, 66 percent are financing college educations with student loans.

   A) True
   B) False

4. Lack of money experience leads many students into serious credit card debt.

   A) True
   B) False

5. Students underestimate or ignore the compounding effect of interest rates and fees on loans as well as credit card debt.

   A) True
   B) False

6. Financial teaching models are taught in most public schools today.

   A) True
   B) False

7. The leading cause of bankruptcy in the 35–44 age group is credit card and student loan debt.

   A) True
   B) False

8. Savings, net worth, and eliminating debt is a priority of the majority of Americans today.

   A) True
   B) False

9. To live the American dream today, parents should do which of the following:

   A) Borrow against their home equity to satisfy wants and desires.
   B) Allow money and emotions to control their lives.
   C) Maximize use of credit cards as a model for their children to follow.
   D) None of the above

Answers: 1-B, 2-A, 3-A, 4-A, 5-A, 6-B, 7-A, 8-B, 9-D

Parental Naivete

Parents have been told, challenged, and convinced that a college education has become more and more important to survive and prosper. It's interesting that the marketing campaigns of various institutions advocate student loans as a way to achieve this. Let's take a little side trip here into Greek history, as it seems today's marketers have read the ancient Greek legend

The Odyssey by Homer. This is a story about the wanderings of Odysseus during the ten years after the fall of Troy.

One of Odysseus's adventures dealt with saving his ship and crew by resisting the call of the Sirens who were luring sailors to their death on rocky coasts with their seductive singing. It appears the marketing folks of today are singing a similar song as the Sirens but substituting seductive incentives, causing many who listen and buy to crash on the rocky shores of debt.

An all-too-common reality in today's world is parents with the best intentions struggling to provide their children with a college education and using student loans to carry the bulk of the financing. Many people believe a college education is a panacea for a future life of prosperity. Too many parents and students blindly as well as emotionally, without long-term planning, take on unwise risks and burden themselves with student loans and credit card debt they will have difficulty repaying.

Many parents of college students who may or may not have graduated are facing long-term student loan repayments, shrinking pocketbooks, and very possibly downgrades in lifestyle. The decision to invest in a college education not only requires a huge commitment on the part of the parents but students as well. As has been said, "Everyone must have some skin in the game."

Short-term and long-term planning must be in play, but in most cases, it is lacking. Of course, there is the thrill of a dream realized, which parents see as giving their kids a head start toward a big future reward. However, one or several misplaced steps or decisions along the way can expose them to the pain of losing it all and drowning in the quicksand of student debt.

If you buy into this philosophy without due diligence before borrowing or investing, you are showing a perilous weakness in your critical thinking skills and financial acumen. This leads to more of the costs of education being shifted onto the backs of eighteen- and nineteen-year-olds who have no clue how much money they'll make in ten or twenty years. They are not concerned about it, as that reality is "in a galaxy far, far away."

Status and Ego

Ingrained in our middle or upper class mind-set is the idea that going, or not going, to the right college may cause a major shift in our lives, the lives of our children, and how we're looked upon by our family, friends, and associates. Let's be realistic: the world will not end, life will go on, and future graduates will survive and prosper if the proper value foundation was instilled during their formative years.

This may come as a surprise, but it doesn't make much difference where your students go to college, it's what they make of the time there that counts. Committed and motivated young adults will do extremely well at whatever school they attend. It's the student who makes the college experience worthwhile, not the college.

A great many students excel at smaller state-supported colleges or universities where the pressure of status is minimized and their interest and confidence can blossom. Most employers are not hung up on where prospective employees received their degree, only that they did so. The important hiring criteria are the amount of industry knowledge, job, and people skills the applicant possesses. Only about 10 percent of business leaders consider where a job applicant went to school to be significant. Obviously, a gap exists between perception and reality, which could be part of the reason more than 45 million Americans are burdened with student loan debt in excess of $1.5 trillion.

If you can afford the prestigious college your child has a burning desire to attend, then by all means, let it be so. However, if you'll have to take on excessive debt through student loans, a second mortgage, or sacrifice of your retirement, you need to rethink the situation, revisit your priorities, and reread the sections on the bad and the ugly of student loans. Realistically, the more expensive school may not be worth the price you and your student will have to pay. Remember, the college does not determines success; the student does.

Doug, now a business owner, explains his pragmatic approach to his college education:

> After spending one year at an expensive college that was paid for with loans, I decided to transfer to a less expensive school and get a job. It wasn't long before I was able to pay off that first year of loans. My older brothers, however, had both stayed at that expensive school and graduated from there. Many years later, they still have large amounts

of debt and will be paying it off for many years to come. That may be one of the best decisions I ever made.

Affordability

Most parents take the short-term view regarding the value of a college education. They willingly take questionable and emotional financial risks, as they want to see their child succeed and earn significant money in a rewarding career. But the successful parents embrace a long-term perspective. They check their egos and impulses at the door and balance competing interests (negative and positive) in a logical, cost-versus-ROI (return on investment) way.

Those who fail to evaluate the investment required and ascertain the level of high-demand skills needed to obtain higher-paying jobs in the future are now, or will be, stuck with the long-term burden of suffocating debt. Additionally, I contend that those students, more than likely with their parents' blessings, were focusing on the college experience rather than career enhancement. In the process of just engaging in the college experience, many acquired, or are acquiring, low-demand skills leading to low-paying jobs, making it impossible to pay off debt quickly and easily.

Expectations

Many parents today, whether they are in a lower- or middle-income bracket, are faced with either the dilemma or opportunity of sending their kids to college. One of the key factors of those in a lower- or middle-income bracket will be their ability to shift their mind-set and think on a higher level, thereby expecting higher results. Or put another way: your expectations will determine your results.

The top 10 to 15 percent of the income-generating population continue to see their financial status and income grow, and I'm sure they're not too concerned about these issues. We might want to ask ourselves why this is and explore the possibility of what they're doing right that we are not. More than likely, we would discover what they are doing has more to do with their level of thinking, their degree of expectations, and the people they associate with than their IQ. You may need to lower your sights regarding your children attending a prestigious, high-cost college.

However, you don't have to lower your expectations on their receiving a quality education. The benefits to be gained from a quality two-year community college or a four-year state-supported school will be comparable to any other school provided your attitude, mind-set, and ego will permit you to allow your children to attend these schools. They will receive value if you expect and demand value.

A point to keep in mind on the value of attending a two-year community college: it may make it easier to get into the four-year college of choice, especially if the community college has a transfer agreement with that college and certain academic requirements are met. Many students are not clearly focused on their future career after completing high school, and a two-year community college could help them define their career goals as well as provide a great way to transition into college-level academics. Two years spent completing required courses at a community college could make a big difference in the overall cost of a college education.

An Ounce of Prevention

In today's society, with information available as never before, it is unconscionable that so many parents fail to plan for their children's college education. In too many cases, parents wait until the last minute to begin any kind of planning at all. Let's take a look at what the future has in store for an average family expecting to send three children to college over the next several years.

Cost projections and schedules are for a four-year degree at a midsize Midwestern state university based on 2017's per year cost of $17,300 per student and factoring in a cost increase of 6 percent per year. Here's how that breaks down for each of the children in this family:

- Child #1 is fifteen years old and in tenth grade; will be entering college in 2021 and graduating in 2025. Projected four-year total cost is $84,000.
- Child #2 is twelve years old and in seventh grade; will be entering college in 2024 and graduating in 2028. Projected four-year total cost is $120,000.

- Child #3 is nine years old and in third grade; will be entering college in 2027 and graduating in 2031. Projected four-year total cost is $130,000.
- Total projected cost for all three children is $334,000.

If hopes are for a major university, then costs will be much higher, so plan accordingly. However, this will give you an idea of what to expect and a place to start. As you can see, there will be a lot of challenges ahead if you delay planning for these events.

If you fail to evaluate the investment required and ascertain the level of high-demand skills needed to obtain higher-paying jobs in the future, you could be stuck with the long-term burden of suffocating debt. Students need to focus less on the college experience and more on career enhancement. In the process of just engaging in the college experience, many students acquire low-demand skills that lead to low-paying jobs, making it impossible to pay off debt quickly and easily. Even if student debt is crushing them and possibly their parents, the burden is almost impossible to get out from under. Remember, what you model to your student when you take on debt is exactly what your student will do in the future.

It's interesting how parents want their kids to make top grades and excel at athletics and various activities but ignore or avoid the need to balance those achievements with financial competencies. Many parents willingly spend $1,000 to $10,000 a year on their children's athletic activities, including camps, league fees, tournaments, gear, uniforms, and travel expenses. For the majority—actually 90 percent—of these children, their athletic careers will be over when they go to college. Financial competency, on the other hand, will be in play every day for the rest of their lives. It is important to make sure sports or other activities are balanced with financial education skills that will be useful long after activities end.

Life Is a Business, and You Are Your Business

A local newspaper published a list of upcoming summer camps. Of the 160 camps listed, covering such subjects as sports, science, math, history, leadership, religion, recreation, art, dance, music, and nature, not one involved an introduction to or development of skills in financial education. What a missed opportunity! Life is a business, just as colleges are businesses, and how well you run your business will determine your personal and financial success. Parents need to realign their mind-set from emphasis on participating and winning on the athletic field to giving their kids the opportunity and skills to win on the financial field of life.

Regardless of which career field students are planning for, they still have to deal with life's realities. So impress upon them (and yourself) that they are their own life manager and should treat themselves as the multi-million-dollar empire they truly are. They will become the CEO (chief executive officer), CFO (chief financial officer), and marketing director of their personal businesses and generate income in excess of $2,000,000 during their working years. How effective their individual managerial skills become will determine whether they are in the top 20 percent of personal business owners who succeed or join the 80 percent of those who fail.

When students are clear on the purpose of going to college, have defined long-range plans for reaching the goal, and can maintain focus on the achievement of that goal, it becomes much easier for them (and you) to confront life's challenges. Successful businesses and individuals align their purpose, goals, and action plans with a conscious mind-set embracing the fact that financial problems can be solved by increasing their financial IQ through learning, understanding, and practicing effective money management. Although marketing and sales, products, and customer service play key roles, it is sound financial management that makes the difference.

Understanding personal finance doesn't mean you won't make mistakes or face financial emergencies. However, you can lessen the odds and repair the damage more quickly by knowing and adhering to financial principles. Financial ignorance is costly and can be heartbreaking and stress-inducing, so lessen the risk by learning, practicing, and modeling sound financial management within your family. As the Greek philosopher Zeno put it, "The most important part of learning is to unlearn our errors."

Parents want the best for their children, yet by avoiding long-range planning, they allow themselves and/or their graduate to sink into years of bondage, struggling to pay off student loans and credit card debt. In the United States, the unemployment rate for twenty- to twenty-four-year-olds with bachelor's degrees is almost 8 percent versus 4+ plus percent for the economy as a whole, according to the US Bureau of Labor Statistics.

To avoid becoming a negative statistic, and before deciding on an investment in your student's higher education, call a meeting with all concerned to agree on and develop an exploratory plan. This means seeking out and gathering every bit of information available about the school—costs and benefits, positives as well as negatives. A bachelor's degree may not necessarily get your student a higher-paying white collar job as opposed to the hands-on skilled trades, such as electrician, machinist, welder, automotive technician, or painter.

A point to keep in mind: there is very little difference between lifetime earnings of an average college graduate and a high school graduate who has chosen a skilled trade. Most trades provide training either on the job or through programs at trade schools and junior colleges, where scholarships abound as the student develops skills. Those who select this path rarely have student loans to pay off.

Parents must hold their students accountable for academic performance and career pursuits while under the umbrella of the family. Remember, a worthy purpose of every family is to teach, inspire, and model the best ways to enrich the family's legacy for future generations. It is good to remember that the greatest lesson you can give your kids is to teach them to grow up believing anything is possible. When they see you achieve your goals and dreams, they will learn more about living a successful debt-free life than any academic program can teach them. Those who believe and invest in themselves will achieve greatness in one form or another, and those who feel undeserving won't have any trouble finding mediocrity.

> *You cannot help men permanently by doing for them what they could and should be doing for themselves.*
> *— Abraham Lincoln*

Acquire Knowledge and Budget

Amazingly, there are unlimited opportunities to be seized by enterprising students with initiative, effort, and encouragement from their parents.

However, it is important that students are prepared for the cost realities of attending college so they do not wind up maxing out their credit cards; spending all of their grant, scholarship, and savings; and asking for an emergency loan before the first semester is even over. Consequently, an understanding of money principles and values is critical.

Begin by encouraging your future student to learn basic accounting, budgeting, and investing. These are the key elements to financial success. It's not necessary for you or your student to become an accountant or banker. You may be fortunate to study with and learn from those who have become financially successful and are willing to teach others to do the same. There are many resources, including financial classes offered at local colleges, qualified friends and associates, good self-help books, and the internet. Financial intelligence is just as important as any coursework students may take. If you are willing to make the commitment, there are people waiting to help you succeed. However, you and the future graduate must apply discipline and energy; maximize resources; and focus on the goal, the plan, and the future.

Budgeting is the one area of financial planning that most people avoid. However, it's the one which will pay the greatest dividends, because when you can see and actually know where your money is going, you are in control. It's flawed reasoning to assume you can build a substantial savings, retirement, or college account without knowing exactly what is happening with your money and expenses. Without a budget and plan to guide you and your student, you are gambling with your family's future. And in gambling, the odds always favor the house and not the player. Establish your goals, pay yourself first (savings), and stick like glue to a budget.

Developing a plan to reach a debt-free college education is a major factor in meeting your goal. A plan is like a road map guiding you to the destination, but with the flexibility to adjust to unplanned contingencies. It requires input of the best information available, teamwork, agreement on the goal, communication, and a commitment to persist until it is accomplished.

Tuition and Fees

Few costs have risen as quickly as that of obtaining a college education. According to *US News and World Report*, in the last ten years, average tuition costs have risen 80 percent, or triple the rate of inflation, twice as much as health care, and four times as much as housing in the same period. As the cost of tuition continues to increase, less is known about where that money goes and how it is used by colleges and universities—but colleges' facilities have certainly improved. They compete by offering things like luxurious swimming pools and gourmet dining, items not known to enhance a résumé for students seriously planning to get a good-paying job.

Tuition, fees, and aid programs at most of these schools usually have a complex structure which isn't always transparent and is rarely simple. Explaining which costs are covered by endowments and donations versus the costs covered by your tuition are confusing. As these items will be included in the overall debt, parents and students, who are the customers, should know exactly where their money goes. The issue is one of fairness and transparency helping to determine and assess whether this school is the right investment and fit for the results expected.

One ongoing concern is the rising cost of student athletics and its impact on tuition costs. Although they're a cash cow for some colleges, most college sports programs see zero revenue and high costs. Such negative results must be considered by every prospective and current college student—specifically how it could impact future additions to tuition and fees.

Sports programs aren't the only college expense that has risen sharply in recent years. Administrative costs and a reliance on expensive adjunct professors have increased as well, not always with the corresponding benefit of improving the instructional model. These are key reasons to know exactly where tuition and fee money go. Students should make responsible decisions about their future and hold colleges and universities accountable to do the same. Rarely does a winning football or basketball program improve a student's career opportunities and quality of life and reduce dependence on student loans, unless the student in question is on a full athletic scholarship and is drafted by the pros.

Hidden Agendas

In addition to the tuition and fees previously mentioned, most educational institutions promoting student loans receive fees and incentives from lenders, just as they do from companies allowed to promote credit cards on campus. These fees have become profit centers for many schools of higher learning. Student loans for these institutions are strictly a money-generating business—a profit center. The students or their guardians are only another number contributing to the bottom line.

Keep in mind that the interest of the college or university is not always the best interest of the students. You must conduct your own due diligence and approach the process like they do, as a business. To get personal clarity on the issue of loans and credit card programs on campus, you should ask the following questions of the college administration before enrolling your future graduate:

Quiz Time

1. Do any of the student loan programs contribute fees or income back to the college for those applicants signed?

   A) Yes
   B) No

2. Does the college endorse credit card companies taking applications from students on campus?

   A) Yes
   B) No

3. Is the college or any campus organization compensated by card companies for this privilege and if so, is there short-term and long-term compensation paid to the college as well?

   A) Yes
   B) No

4. As a part of that deal with the college, are those credit card companies provided with the names and addresses of the student population?

   A) Yes
   B) No

5. Is any of that money received used for scholarships, grants, and financial education in order to benefit those who pay tribute to the card companies?

   A) Yes
   B) No

6. What personal financial programs are required and being taught to help students understand and manage their finances in a responsible manner?

   _____
   _____

7. Is credit counseling available?

   A) Yes
   B) No

8. If members of the administration, were preparing to send a son or daughter to college, what would be their approach and plan to insure their student graduates with minimum debt?

   _____
   _____

Credit Cards 101

> *Why don't somebody print the truth about our present economic condition? We spent years of wild buying on credit, everything under the sun, whether we needed it or not, and now we are having to pay for it, and we are howling like a pet coon. This would be a great world to dance in, if we didn't have to pay the fiddler.* — Will Rogers

Marketing by loan companies encouraging people to solve their financial challenges and fulfill their desires through the use of credit cards is relentless. They've made it easy to obtain credit cards and "only" require minimum monthly payments coupled with high interest rates and excessive fees, which allow the lenders to earn extraordinary profits. Those high profits have led to a lessening of lending standards, making credit cards available to poorer risks.

According to the Federal Reserve, those companies' fees and interest (charged to the borrower) generated in excess of $160 billion in income for 2016. The average US household credit card debt is projected to be over $16,000 for 2018, representing almost 25 percent of total household debt, with mortgages and car payments making up the balance.

Many individuals have a need to express themselves with material items, as that's how they define their lives. Inwardly, it's the psychological factors involved in creating the mind-set to buy and charge today with a false sense of being able to pay off the cards easily tomorrow. Some people, because of circumstances, are using credit cards just to survive. They're using them for groceries, housing, and living expenses because of a shortage of income in their household budgets. They're caught up in a whirlpool that is dragging them further down into a state of debt, and unbelievably, the credit card companies are rewarding them for this behavior, especially seniors, minorities, and other poor money managers.

Most borrowers miscalculate their use of credit cards, the impact of the interest rates and fees, and their ability to pay off the balances. They avoid as well as fail to read and understand the disclosure statement information with their credit cards. This lists and states in small print the various fees that will be charged as well as the factors which will trigger an increase in your interest rate. It's a double-barreled credit gun that can bring you to your knees as effectively as any weapon if you choose to ignore the fine print with many of the same conditions as student loans.

That's why you've got to pay more than the minimum. The goal of the credit card company is to get you to not pay as much as you want to because the less you pay, the longer it goes, and the longer it goes, the more interest they make on you. That's what they're in business to do.

As Will Rogers described it in his day, "This Country right now is operating on a Dollar down and a Dollar a Week. It ain't Taxes that is hurting this Country; it's Interest." And now, excessive and hidden fees charged to credit card users could be added to this quote. Credit card companies have saturated the adult market with offers and now have penetrated college enrollments with very persuasive marketing. According to the Demos Report "Students in Debt; Credit Cards on Campus," more than 75 percent of undergraduates have credit cards. The average student has more than one card and a debt exceeding $2,500.

Students have seen how their parents use credit cards, and they, too, want to have material goods. Lending companies have learned to capitalize on these traits, and through promotions and special offers, they encourage students to follow suit. Many undergraduates, because of a lack of money, experience, and financial education, have allowed themselves to be drawn into serious debt compounded with student loans. One higher education administrator at a major college recently was heard saying, "We lose more students to credit card debt than academic failure."

Factor in any credit card debt, its interest and fees, and tomorrow's graduates will be starting their career with a heavy load to carry on an uphill climb. Instead of paying for college in four years, now it's taking an average of fifteen years, according to the US Department of Education. Those graduates looking forward to new careers in what should be their most productive years are now facing mounting debt, slower economic growth, and underemployment.

The credit card companies' aggressive marketing geared to students' lack of money experience and financial education has led many undergraduates into serious debt compounded by their student loans. Most students (and parents) avoid reading and understanding the disclosure information with their credit card information. This fine print lists the fees you can be charged and ways the card companies can raise your interest rates.

> *They hope we buy and charge so they can have the glory.*
> *— Unknown*

Credit Card Strategy

One family issued strict guidelines to their student on the use of credit cards: "If you can eat it or drink it, wear it or hear it, you cannot charge it to your card." This is good advice for all of us.

Various reporting agencies indicate the average household in the United States with credit card debt pays out of their family budget in excess of $2,000 in interest fees and late charges every year plus principle. By reducing and eliminating credit card debt, the average family would have an additional $2,000 plus per year to contribute to their students' college education. Always ask yourself the following question when tempted to use that credit card: "What's really important here, this self-satisfying purchase or my children's education?"

Many parents take a realistic approach when introducing kids to credit cards, usually around their junior year in high school, outlining specific rules they must adhere to in order to keep the card. These rules include only having one credit card, paying it off in full every month, and absolutely no carry-over charges to allow interest to build. Along with this would be the requirement to work within a budget, including figuring monthly income and determining allowable expenses, such as clothes, gas, and specifically needed items. Key points stressed constantly are the importance of savings, working, and earning.

When it comes time to leave the nest and move away, these young people will have learned to take personal responsibility to manage their own income, adjusting for expenses like utilities, water, and phone bills along with insurance and groceries Because they have gained an understanding of money matters—including how to manage income and expenses, make responsible purchases, diligently pay off credit card balances, save money, and live within their means—their future will look much brighter, and the American dream will be within reach.

Responsible credit card usage requires a disciplined, unwavering, and committed approach in order to achieve one's savings goals. Be the teacher and the student who does the homework. A student is one who studies, investigates, asks questions, and becomes skilled at making responsible choices. Remember that fees, increasing interest rates, and compounding interest make up a triple-barreled debt gun that can bring parents and students to their knees as effectively as any weapon if they choose to charge indiscriminately on their credit cards and ignore the fine print. Here's a simple little rule to keep in mind: You *can* leave home without your credit cards!

The Fine Print

As an example, a recent credit card application from American Express included the following fine print:

> The introductory APR'S (annual percentage rates) and any other promotional rates will terminate upon your account being considered in default or seriously in default and the applicable Default APR will apply. We may apply payments and credits first to your balances with lower APRs (including balances with promotional APRs) before balances with higher APRs. This will result in the lower APR balances being paid before the higher APR balances.
>
> The terms of your account including APRs, are subject to change. The APRs for this offer are not guaranteed; APRs may change to higher APRs, fixed APRs may change to variable APRs, or variable APRs may change to fixed APRs. We may change the terms (including APRs) at any time for any reason in addition to APR increases for failure to comply with the terms of your account."

You'll notice there isn't any fine print in this book like that on the disclosure statements of your credit card, prescription information, or student loan papers. What you see here and can easily read without a magnifying glass is what you get. There are no disclaimers, harmful side effects, increases in interest rates, add-ons, additional fees, or repercussions involved if you fail to read and understand what I'm saying. Your life will not change because you choose not to read this book, but it can change, and not necessarily for the better, if you fail to read, ignore, or understand the fine print on those listed items.

Note that grace periods for payments are a thing of the past. If you are one day, one hour, or one minute late, you may be considered in default, and the higher APRs will kick in. Now you go from a prime rate to a prime rate plus 21.99 percent on your credit card balance. How will that impact your budget and ability to pay off this debt?

Teachable Moments

Understand the importance of your role in teaching your kids the value of responsibility, hard work, and self-sufficiency while they are growing up. At times, tough love must play a role in children's upbringing, instilling the importance of learning to earn at an early age, discipline in one's actions, and the value of saving for that rainy day. Other principles to live by, to be taught and modeled in the home, include honesty, gratitude, and tolerance, along with keeping your word and honoring your family and obligations. Lessons taught and embraced at a young age will pay off later.

IQ is less a predictive indicator of a student's future success in life than character-building traits like persistence, optimism, curiosity, and self-control, which greatly influence one's chances of eventually living the American dream. Remember, the greatest influence in children's lives as a predictor of success is what they see and hear in the home and whether or not it is coupled with a nurturing relationship. (The second greatest influence is their teachers.) Are you living and modeling what you are advocating? This is important and may need to be addressed immediately.

Are you afraid to deny your children frivolous and expensive gadgets that do not help them develop financial awareness and self-reliance for upcoming challenges? Does your monthly cell or iPhone, internet, and cable bill exceed your weekly grocery budget? Are your children helping to pay for any of those services they are using? If not, more than likely you will continue to buy those items by yielding to pressure from your kids, adding to your credit card debt, and making yourself a negative role model they will emulate in their own lives. Your children will allow you to go broke supporting them if you don't have the courage to engage in tough love by setting expectations, saying no, and refusing to enable them.

What's the Cost?

> *It matters not how strait the gate,*
> *How charged with punishment the scroll,*
> *I am the Master of my Fate;*
> *I am the Captain of my Soul.*
>
> — *W. E. Henley,* Invictus

Let's have another reality check here before we go any further. Learning is our business, and we cannot ignore or avoid the fact that we make the choices and decisions leading us into, or away from, debt. How we exercise our personal responsibility and accountability for what we do is the determining cause of our success or failure as money managers and role models for our children. Life is a business, and you are your business.

According to Alan Greenspan, "In many respects, improving financial education at the elementary and secondary school level is essential to providing a foundation for financial literacy that can help prevent younger people from making poor financial decisions that can take years to overcome." The truth of Greenspan's words can be seen in the number of homeless people, including former student loan borrowers and veterans, who are on the streets and in shelters because of bad decisions and choices from a lack of financial education and sound practices. Money mismanagement, as reported by a substantial number of veterans and confirmed in studies by the Department of Veterans Affairs, has led a higher rate of subsequent homelessness. The findings have implications for policymakers and clinicians, suggesting that financial education programs offered by the US Departments of Defense and Veterans Affairs may effectively address veteran homelessness.

Be a Pragmatist First

Let me recap. It is important for you and your future college graduate to understand completely that you are your business and going to school requires a businesslike approach if the goal is to acquire a debt-free education in the pursuit of a fulfilling and rewarding career. When students are clear on their purpose for going to college, have a defined plan for reaching that goal, and can maintain their focus on the achievement of that goal, it becomes much easier for them (and you) to confront the challenges that inevitably show up.

Successful businesses and individuals align their purpose, goals, and action plans with a mind-set embracing the fact that financial problems can be solved by increasing one's financial IQ through learning, understanding, and practicing effective money management. Although marketing and sales, products, and customer service play key roles, it is sound financial management that makes the difference. Regardless of the career field, your student will still have to deal with life's realities. So impress upon your children (and yourself) that they are their own life manager and should consider and care for themselves as the multimillion-dollar empire they truly are or will become.

The value of a college education should be determined by whether it is worth the initial financial cost that will generate the long-term benefits desired. Insist that, with your assistance, your student calculate the projected difference in salary expected from the preferred career field versus how many years it will take to recoup the cost of a college education. This will be a giant step in positive decision-making and extremely important if student loans are considered.

If students assume 100 percent of their own financial support, then it's time to cut the umbilical cord, releasing them to pursue their own destiny. Until that day arrives, help them decide whether their goal is worth the ROI. When we talk about investing in a college education, it must be understood between the parent and student that this requires both parties to be vested in the effort, with each doing their share. If parents contribute, so must the student.

What are those approximate costs, and how should they be met? The following example of a realistic and doable plan is based on a conservative estimate of projected cost for a four-year degree at a midsize Midwestern state university in 2018. The per-year in-state cost is estimated at $18,000 per student and adjusted upward 6 percent every year thereafter. You will need to adjust the cost figures depending upon the college or university preferred. Let's create a plan and plan to win.

> *Every well-built house started with a definite plan in the form of blueprints.* — Napoleon Hill

Now that we have an idea of approximately how much college is going to cost, it's time to focus on building up a substantial savings and investment fund to meet those obligations. The plan needs to clarify how costs and expenses are to be met, who is to share (percentage and/or dollar amounts) in the financial responsibility to meet the obligation, and where the money is coming from. Money sources should be a combination of scholarships, grants, savings, and job earnings. Financial aid (student loans), which requires payback after graduation, *should not* be included.

Now let's divide the projected cost up into proportional shares, with each part assigned to its respective contributor. There are many variables and combinations that can be used, and the following is only one of many possibilities.

Proposed Division of Cost

(Always subject to circumstances, initiative, and efforts.)

45% student working, full-time and part-time	$ 8,100
15% student savings	$ 2,700
20% grants/scholarships	$ 3,600
20% parents	$ 3,600
100% total	$18,000

Assuming graduation takes place in four years, the total cost would be $78,743, divided as follows:

45% student working, full-time and part-time	$35,434
15% student savings	$11,811
20% grants/scholarships	$15,749
20% parents	$15,749
100% total	$78,743

Motivated students who are willing to do their part, put in the effort, and add to their work résumé should have no trouble earning $12,000–$15,000 per year for their efforts. Weeks available for full-time work include thirteen to fourteen in the summer, three at semester break, and one at spring break. That's seventeen weeks, forty hours a week, at a minimum of $9 per hour equals $6,120. There are thirty weeks during the school year (two semesters) available for part-time work. Working at least twenty-five hours a week, earning $9 per hour, equals $6,750, for a total of $12,870 minimum per school year. A key component of the budget has been achieved for the first year.

If this schedule seems too demanding, reread the sections on the bad and the ugly of student loans and consider this: There are many students seeking a degree who are working full-time and attending classes in the evening, weekends, and online. In many cases, their employer is providing tuition reimbursement, and they will graduate debt-free. Remember, life is a business, and how well you run that business determines the level of success you achieve.

Would a prospective employer be impressed with a student who is goal-oriented, committed to do what it takes, and willing to make personal sacrifices to achieve the objective? An individual capable of stepping up to life's challenges and work in different environments with a variety of individuals? Someone eager to acquire team-building and business skills, all while gaining the self-confidence to take charge of their own destiny? Does this not demonstrate maturity, responsibility, purpose, and resolve?

> *The way to wealth, if you desire it, is as plain as the way to the market. It depends chiefly on two words, industry and frugality; that is waste neither time nor money, but make the best use of both.* — Benjamin Franklin

The student has the most to gain in the long term; therefore, the student should be required and willing to put in the biggest investment. There are many variations and options as well as adjustments that may be needed along the way. However, the goal is to pay as you go and avoid any long-term burden for either party. This is where the lessons of financial life really begins.

Cosigning

Up to now, the emphasis has been on understanding the risks and consequences associated with student loans, which can very well derail your and your student's aspirations if due diligence is ignored. However, if it is determined student loans are necessary and you are considering cosigning with your student, you need to understand this up front: cosigned debt is 100 percent *your* debt. If the primary borrower defaults, declares bankruptcy, becomes disabled, or dies, the debt will be yours to pay. So ask yourself this question: "If this person wasn't family, would I do business with them?"

Parents should ask themselves the following questions about their children:

- How are they at resolving conflict?
- If they get into trouble, will they cut and run, leaving me holding the bag, or will they work with me to honor their obligations?
- Do they have a strong sense of responsibility for their actions and decisions?
- Do they care how this might affect me?
- Can they be depended on to do the right thing?
- Can I really afford, financially and emotionally, to go into business with them?

After all, who better to know their history, values, and sense of loyalty than the ones who raised them?

When you cosign for a family member, there is a certain level of trust built into the relationship. You are putting your faith in the future. You have faith this person will be around and always have your best interests at heart. Unfortunately, oftentimes people will take advantage of others, whether family, friends, or colleagues. Although you don't think your kid isn't going to pay, be realistic, as you have a lot at risk.

Before you cosign, understand that in the event your student is one of the 25 percent of graduates who default on their loans, you are the one at risk. Will you be financially able to make these payments, which may range from $500 to $1,200 per month, for the next ten to twenty years? When it comes to money issues, people can get scared, choose to hide under a rock, disappear, or ignore the problem as if it does not exist. Understand that if you are the cosigner, meaning the guarantor, you have guaranteed repayment, and the lender will want its due regardless of personal circumstances.

After graduation, the primary borrower can apply for cosigner release after making twelve consecutive monthly on-time principal and interest payments. Sallie Mae looks very carefully at the primary borrower's demonstrated success with other credit obligations (such as car payments, apartment rent, or credit cards) when considering whether this individual has sufficient income to take over the payments. If the primary borrower meets the stringent credit criteria, the cosigner may be released from the loan obligation, but don't bank on it.

For those age sixty-five to seventy-four, education loans amounted to 13 percent of all installment debt in 2010, according to the most recent figures available from the Federal Reserve. In 2007, the last time the survey was conducted, the level was so low that it wasn't disclosed. As that debt burden rises, older people are having a tougher time repaying. More than 2.2 million Americans sixty years of age or older owe in excess of $43 billion in student loans, and more than 10 percent of those loan balances are at least ninety days delinquent. For fifty- to fifty-nine-year-olds, the numbers are rising rapidly. In many cases, grandparents are pulled into the debt quagmire by cosigning when a student's own parents don't qualify.

Financial gurus predict that given the rate student debt is growing along with the state of the economy, as well as those parents approaching retirement, cosigning problems are likely to escalate. The federal government usually doesn't require cosigners for the loans it makes to students. But if the economy weakens, banks will step up their demands for cosigners on private loans, especially those often made to families who have already maxed out on federal loans. All told, more than 90 percent of private loans had cosigners last year, according to the Consumer Financial Protection Bureau, up from 67 percent in 2008.

Many parents are facing financial pressures they never expected, from adult kids moving back home (28 percent of graduates) to their own parents who may be dealing with medical issues. Now a new headache is affecting their lifestyle: cosigned student loans. Thinking it was only natural to help their children, large numbers of parents have become the latest victims of this nation's mounting student-loan debt problem. Before you sign on the dotted line, I suggest you seriously consider the following: in the event the unthinkable happens—such as the student becoming disabled or dying—you will not be released from paying off the debt. So take out a term life and disability insurance policy on your child with you as the beneficiary.

People who need cosigners need them because the lender believes they're a bad risk. By the way, have you heard of anyone with a good cosigning experience? For cosigners, when the primary borrower defaults, the consequences are severe. Defaulted loans show up on their credit reports as if the debt was theirs. Even if loans are current, the additional debt makes it tougher for cosigners to qualify for other loans, such as mortgage refinancing. When confronted by the lender to pay up for someone else's bad decision, many older people feel they have no choice but to tap into savings or retirement accounts to fulfill their obligations.

Here's where tough love comes in. It's not worth sacrificing or risking your future, home, savings, or retirement income. You probably earned your rewards the old-fashioned way: by working, sacrificing, and saving. So what's wrong with that plan?

Even if a student is able to induce a parent to cosign for a student loan, it is important students do their part to justify the investment by working, saving, and contributing their own money in the pursuit of a degree of which they will be the primary beneficiary. A doable and logical degree plan outlining strengths, weaknesses, financial contribution, and commitment to follow through is essential.

> *Better to go to bed supperless, than to wake up in debt.*
> — Benjamin Franklin

Plan to Win

The following is one example of what can happen when a couple of guys have a dream to accomplish a goal, believe in the power of affirmation, are persistent in the pursuit of that goal, and refuse to give up.

A Master Plan in Action

I was fortunate to be a part of, although indirectly, one of the most significant events ever to take place in the literary field of book publishing and marketing. Early in 1993, a speaker, trainer, and entrepreneur of some renown came to our church to do a program and gave a living example of how a master plan can propel one to phenomenal success.

He and a fellow speaker had been encouraged to write a book comprised of the many inspirational stories they had shared with their audiences over the years. They began putting the book together and at the same time created a master plan on how they would bring this book to millions of readers around the world. Their belief was so strong in the value of this book that they willingly made the commitment, without hesitation or doubt, to follow their master plan and do whatever it took to promote and sell the message of inspiration, hope and prosperity included in their book.

On this day in church, the soon-to-be author extraordinaire stood on the platform in front of four hundred members of the congregation holding the final manuscript in his hand and stated his intention. He asked those of us in attendance to hold in our hearts, our minds, and our prayers that we see this book in every bookstore, airport, church, and library in the country. By asking others to support their intention through words and deeds, which was a part of their master plan, the authors stayed motivated and focused enough to follow through and do those things necessary to bring their dream into reality.

It wasn't easy, but they persevered, even as the book was rejected by more than thirty publishers. It was finally published later that year by a company that decided to take a chance because of the authors' commitment, perseverance, and strength of purpose. After the printing of that first book, supported by the marketing and promotional efforts of the authors, a brand evolved, leading to a whole series of books that to date have sold over 500,000,000 copies worldwide. The book was *Chicken Soup for the Soul*, and its authors are Jack Canfield and Mark Victor Hansen.

For a plan to work, it must be carried out as a team so that everyone in the family is aligned and focused on achieving the same goals and objectives. The team concept also clarifies each family member's role and responsibility for meeting the goals. It helps everyone to maintain a clear, focused approach as the plan is created, is put into play, and brings results. Remember, no one is an island, and every family member's contribution is just as important as the next.

It is important that students participate, contribute, and make a personal and financial investment in their college education. This means they need to step up and assume their share of responsibility and accountability, and parents should not assume all the risk and responsibility for the funding. These are important lessons preparing students to confidently face the reality of life after college.

There must be continual follow up (review sessions) to make sure the plan is being carried out and is on target. This is very important, as it is easy to get sidetracked and focused on day-to-day activities and lose sight of the goal, which is a debt-free college education. Everyone must understand that being effective and reaching the goal involves time, commitment, defined responsibilities, constant communication, and continual effort. Post the plan where it can be reviewed daily along with progress results in moving toward each goal. This goal is not about money but what money will allow you to do: achieve a debt-free college education for your student.

> *Poverty and riches often change places. When riches take the place of poverty, the change is usually brought about through well-conceived and carefully executed plans. Poverty needs no plan. It needs no one to aid it, because it is bold and ruthless. Riches are shy and timid. They have to be "attracted."*
> — *Napoleon Hill*

Make It a Family Affair

Convene close members of the family, including grandparents, to map out the future cost of a college education and create a doable plan—the sooner the better. Ask family members to contribute to special tax-preferred college funds while there is time for the fund to appreciate. The donation may be tax deductible.

As a suggestion, look at a Coverdell Education Savings Account, a state sponsored 529 college savings plan, and/or a Roth IRA. Just make sure the investment fund meets your long-term needs and not the needs of the broker. Don't allow yourself to be guided into a fund or plan loaded with commission and management fees, or you'll find less in the plan than you invested when it comes time to pay for that college education.

Also, set up your own family scholarship program with every member of the family contributing. What a great way for a family to support each other in regular and measurable ways. Remember, this would be a no-load, no-fee program, and the primary requirement is discipline and a strict adherence to the plan.

Discuss Money and Success Topics at the Dinner Table

> *A single conversation across the table with a wise man is worth a month's study of books.*   — Chinese proverb

Have special evening dinners, beginning in the elementary grades and continuing through high school, with all family members present, openly and freely discussing money issues ranging from earning, saving, investing, and dealing with the everyday financial challenges of life. Include everyone in the discussion. Take a nonjudgmental position, as the purpose is to learn from and support each other in building a solid base of financial understanding.

Side note: As an additional benefit and perhaps the most important one, studies are showing that children who eat meals with their families on a regular basis are healthier and less likely to smoke, drink, or use drugs than those who don't. The children's accomplishments seem to increase more positively, with a corresponding decrease in behavioral problems. So it's important to set aside three or four times a week to have family meals together and make them special and positive.

For variety, have each person present a particular topic or issue for discussion. This is also a great time to talk about inspirational individuals and how they achieved success and made a difference in their lives as well as the world around them by practicing the values and principles of success. Key into your children's interest and focus on successful people they can relate to. Ask them to do the same and share with you the ideas and ways these people achieved success.

> *If you can tell me who your heroes are, I can tell you how you're going to turn out in life.*   — Warren Buffet

Commitment

Make a heartfelt commitment of time and energy to assist your student in acquiring a college education debt-free. Express your willingness to put forth the effort to make the goal a reality. Once the commitment is made, acquire an understanding of basic accounting and investing principles, if needed, and practice them with a passion. As Goethe writes, "Until one is committed, there is hesitancy, the chance to draw back. Whatever you can do, or dream you can do, begin it. Boldness has genius, power, and magic in it. Begin it now."

If parents are committed to the development of their children and engage in open communication practices which allow each family member to be heard, then understanding and respect is the result. An important benefit is the growth of children's self-esteem when they feel they are accepted, appreciated, and valued by their parents. This period in early childhood development is the foundation of later success as adults. It is within the family where children learn about values, conflict resolution, effective communication, and finding their own sense of worth.

Be consistent in the attitude and feelings you inwardly embrace about achievement and money, such as, "I don't accept or project self-limiting beliefs." Make sure they are the same ones you outwardly express to your children and others. For example, when your child or future college student asks for something, how often have you said, "We can't afford it!" Whether you realize it or not, that's a negative statement, and a limiting belief is planted into that child's thoughts. Turn the negative statement into a positive question and present it this way: "If this is really important to you, how can we afford it without debt?"

Now brainpower and creative thinking are brought into play in coming up with the best way to solve the problem of affordability. This also causes students to look at wants versus needs more critically in terms of value and then decide how important it is in their lives at this moment and what effort is required to get it. This is a great long-term lesson that will prove invaluable later on in their lives—provided you practice consistency in its application.

> *If you treat an individual ... as if he were what he ought to be and could be, he will become what he ought to be and could be.*
> — Goethe

Quiz Time

1. Effective teamwork defines each member's role and responsibility.

    A) True
    B) False

2. Which of the following is important to the success of a team approach?

   A) Time commitment
   B) Focusing on the goal
   C) Communication and commitment
   D) Continual and consistent effort
   E) All of the above

3. We all set goals to achieve our dreams.

   A) True
   B) False

4. The primary focus of a goal is all about money.

   A) True
   B) False

5. A financial plan for college needs to begin

   A) When a student is a senior in high school.
   B) With the freshman year of high school.
   C) As soon as possible.
   D) None of the above

6. To be effective, family discussions need to be

   A) Open and honest.
   B) About the realities of everyday money issues.
   C) About inspirational individuals' successes.
   D) All of the above

7. Commitment requires a willingness and determination to make the effort to succeed.

   A) True
   B) False

8. Attitudes and words projecting a limiting belief on a child help to develop a confident young adult.

   A) True
   B) False

Answers: 1. A; 2. E; 3. B; 4. B; 5. C; 6. D; 7. A; 8. B.

Planning to win is a team effort focused on accomplishing a specific goal, which is to achieve a debt-free college education with your student. It requires open and positive discussion on money issues, effective communication, and the willingness to make a commitment to succeed. Attitude, values, and sensible modeling by parents on controlling income and debt will prove invaluable throughout the student's college experience, personal life, and career. As Booker T. Washington wrote, "Few things help an individual more than to place responsibility upon him, and to let him know that you trust him."

Modeling and Mentoring for Results

> *Our children certainly do not lack ability, only good role models and teachers.* — Charley Green

One of our challenges as concerned parents is to model responsible money competency in our own affairs in a positive way for our children to emulate. When we set the standard through example, personal leadership, and practicing what we preach, they will follow our lead. I often read about folks who've influenced others and been role models, even those from the past who show up in various stories and fables. We are going to visit some of those I found inspirational and even applicable to an existing situation or two.

The Man of La Mancha

The musical version includes the song "The Impossible Dream" and is one of my favorites. I could see myself partnered with Don Quixote, portraying his sidekick, Sancho. I like Don Quixote's attitude because he exhibits no fear while pursuing lofty dreams, sees opportunity in every situation, and rights wrongs. Sancho, although hesitant and questioning Don Quixote's purpose and common sense at times, goes along because he believes in the man. And, in the end, Sancho becomes more than he had ever thought possible. Now that's a dream worth living.

Joshua and Gideon

Stay with me as we take a little journey down biblical lane, demonstrating how modeling and mentoring played out for a couple of my favorite biblical heroes, Joshua and Gideon. These could be considered metaphors or maybe lessons to embrace and can be related to the situations we talk about here in this book. You might just see yourself in one of these characters or situations, possibly relating to parenting and/or student loans and their burdensome debt. A little background information first.

Folks often relate America to the land of opportunity, the biblical version of the promised land. The promised land is the land of milk and honey—a land of peace, love, civility, and prosperity. It's the land where our visions and dreams reside, waiting for us to bring them to life.

I like the story of the promised land for the meaning it gives to today's opportunities as well as the lessons it teaches us about what it takes to fulfill our dreams and reach the promised land. The following is from a little book of mine titled *The Journey of Charley and Gideon to the Promised Land*. I have taken a bit of literary license with these two stories; however, I've remained true to the spirit and essence of the lesson to help make the point.

For a lot of folks, getting to the promised land isn't easy; they've got to cross many barriers, just as the Israelites did when Moses led them out of Egypt and up to the banks of the Jordan River. The Jordan represented the border of and the gateway to the promised land. However, the Israelites remained in the wilderness for forty years without crossing over the Jordan, suffering the trials and hardships of that existence.

Why did they not cross? Because they were apprehensive, scared, and not mentally or spiritually prepared. Their challenge was to find ways to overcome those mental blocks, or as I will call it, the fear of change and success. Some things haven't changed from those times. It's the same today, as many people want the glory and the rewards of the promised land but few are willing to make the commitment, effort, and sacrifices to get there.

Now, most of us have heard of Joshua and the battle of Jericho. However, not a lot of people know of Joshua's journey. Joshua followed Moses out of Egypt, became his intern, and spent the next forty years in the wilderness with the Israelites not only just surviving, enduring hardships, and overcoming challenges but also using his time to learn, meditate, plan, and dream of the day he might become leader of the Israelites.

When that day arrived, Joshua was ready. His mission, and he decided to accept it, was to lead the Israelites out of the wilderness, across the Jordan River, and into the promised land—the land of milk and honey, civility, love, and prosperity. When Joshua took command, he stood on a tall rock before 40,000 Israelites and possibly said, "I have a plan! In three days, we'll cross over the Jordan River into the promised land and claim our goods." And so they did.

This promptness of action by Joshua was the result of having an inspiring mentor, Moses, who guided him in the development of his faith, confidence, and inner power. It was Moses who taught the slaves they had an inner power that would deliver them from bondage and wilderness experiences. However, it was Joshua who helped them externalize that inner power through action and use it to claim their promised land, settle there permanently, and pass on the vast wealth they created to future generations.

Joshua ruled over the Israelites for ten years before passing away. After he died, the Israelites returned to their old ways and old patterns, ignoring God's commandments and worshiping false idols. Needless to say, the Lord was a bit peeved and began to punish them for their disobedience. He brought upon them seven years of oppression under the rule of the Midianites. These Midianites were from the land of Midian, and their soldiers represented fear, negative thoughts, and forgiveness issues.

The Midianites ravaged the Israelites' land, forcing them to live in mountain caves and strongholds, just barely surviving, under miserable conditions. They were aimless, hopeless, and homeless. (Just like many who are suffering under the burden of student debt today.)

The Lord reached out and chose Gideon, a poor farm boy, to lead the Israelites against the Midianites. However, Gideon hadn't been trained by Moses, and he was a bit overwhelmed by the task he was being asked to pursue. Gideon needed the support and guidance of a powerful role model—one who understood his fears and stayed by his side, supporting him all the way, even when Gideon was questioning his own abilities, courage, and faith.

His mentor, the Lord, said to him, "I will be with you and we will do this together O' Mighty Warrior. Believe that I believe there is greatness within you" (From "The Book of Gideon"). And with support and those encouraging words, Gideon overcame his fears and achieved victory over the Midianites. The Israelites, under his rule, enjoyed prosperity for the next forty years.

Joshua was a strategist, organizer, and advocate of what Bill Gove (regarded as "the father of professional speaking") has described as "the power of positive doing." Joshua believed in being prepared when his moment to make a difference arrived. He was able to lead the Israelites into the promised land because he knew his purpose and what he was there to do. He asked for guidance, sought out the best mentors available, and trained with them. He wasn't a lone wolf. Joshua listened, learned, applied, and executed with decisiveness and courage.

He set specific goals, meditated on them, and visualized success. When he took action, he was clear about his goal; he was prepared and focused. Joshua had a well thought-out step-by-step strategy, with flexibility to adjust to changing circumstances and conditions. He had taken care of himself mentally, emotionally, physically, and spiritually, refusing to be dragged down by himself or others. He was passionate, enthusiastic, committed, and persistent in his efforts to reach his goal.

Gideon, on the other hand, was not prepared when his moment arrived. However, with his mentor's guidance and plan, he was led step by step in overcoming his fear, hesitation, and procrastination, and he consequently led his people out of oppression and back into their promised land. This approach prepared him psychologically to win, accept the greatness within, and receive an abundance of wealth.

However you choose to look at these examples, the point is that we all need to have the best available role models and mentors in our corner helping and guiding us. Whether we realize it or not, we're also role models to our families, our children, and our community of friends. Remember, they're also looking for, or needing, the best help available, so saddle up—we're it.

Taking Command of Income

If you spend more than you make, you are spending your future income. — *James E. Stowers*

Know how money works and make it work for you instead of allowing it to control you. This is really where the education begins, and getting a firm grasp on this concept now will make it easier when your student transitions into that other world we know as real life: the career after college.

Money and Income

> *Industry, perseverance and frugality make fortune yield.*
> — *Benjamin Franklin*

Teach your children that each dollar earned is seed money and is to be used to enhance their financial well-being through saving, investing, and giving. If they fail to plant a portion of their earnings in areas such as savings, tithing, and investments, it will never grow and multiply. And when it's not allowed to grow and multiply, an increased dependency on debt comes into play. The following allegory or fable may give a different perspective on this part.

Parable of the Talents—Matthew 25:14–30

The parable tells of a master who was leaving his home to travel. Before going, he gave his three servants different amounts of money. On returning from his travels, the master asked his servants for an account of the money given to them.

The first servant reported that he had been given five talents and had earned five talents more. The master praised the servant as being good and faithful, gave him more responsibility because of his faithfulness, and invited the servant to celebrate with him.

The second servant said that he had received two talents and had earned two talents more. The master praised this servant in the same way, as being good and faithful. He gave the servant more responsibility and invited the servant to also celebrate with him.

The last servant, who received one talent, had buried his talent in the ground for safekeeping so he could return the original amount to his master. The master called him a lazy servant, saying he should have placed the money in the bank to generate interest. The master commanded that the one talent be taken away and given to the servant with ten talents, because everyone who has much will be given more, and whoever has a little, even the little will be taken away, and so he fired the servant.

The word *talent* here refers to the weight of something of worth, such as gold, but also implies that we should use our skills, abilities, and money wisely and not bury them, which benefits no one. Help your children learn to exercise control over their spending habits and understand the importance of personal accountability for their money down to the penny. Above all, you must teach them how to get by on cash first before they jump into the quicksand of credit. Practicing a cash-only philosophy is the best way to avoid credit card debt.

Rule of Thumb on Income

Teach your children to tithe 10 percent, save/invest 10 percent, spend 10 percent on entertainment, and meet their expenses and obligations with the other 70 percent. This is a good model to adhere to. When practiced consistently, it will lead you and them on the path to abundance into the future.

Remember, the goal is to help future college graduates get an education and earn a degree debt-free. They may not thank you now, as they'll have to do their part; however, after college, they'll be grateful when they begin new careers without the burden of debt. They'll be especially thankful when they notice how many of their friends and their friends' parents who weren't willing to pay the price are now weighted down with a mountain of debt to repay. It all comes down to embracing a winning mind-set requiring the following:

- You gotta want it,
- You gotta plan it, and
- *You* gotta do it!

Spending and Saving

You may not feel comfortable with or competent at balancing a checkbook, but now is the time to get with it, or your children will model your discomfort. They must learn how to read a bank statement, know at all times how much money is in their account, and track what checks have been written that are still outstanding. This means keeping their checkbooks updated by recording all transactions as they occur, entering the various fees that may have been charged, and monitoring their account frequently online or through their bank's call-in system.

A little time spent doing this will certainly help them to stay on track with their budget, avoid overdraft charges, and detect any errors or unauthorized transactions. This way, they remain in control of their finances and can take the guesswork out of whether or not there's money in the account before making an expenditure. You should teach them not only to keep their checkbook balanced at all times but to avoid the use of automated teller machines. If they must use an ATM in an emergency, they should do so with the same bank where their checking account is located.

When it comes to savings, the most effective but toughest way to grow an account is to reduce spending, increase income, and budget wisely. When you are committed to a budget, you know where your money is going, and there will be no surprises at the end of the month when it's time to honor your savings goals and financial obligations. Remember, students who graduate in debt have never learned or practiced good savings habits, and consequently, they will tend to be poor savers in the future. The less money you and your student save today, the greater amount you and they will need to borrow tomorrow.

You should always choose a saving vehicle with the shortest compounding period and the highest interest rate offered. As previously stated, compound interest is when a specified interest rate is applied to the original principle and any accumulated interest to date. In essence, it is interest paid on interest. Compound interest has a significant effect over the long term, and as the interest rate increases, daily compounding—which will work 24/7 for you—has a greater impact on your savings and investments than compounding monthly or annually.

The three key areas to focus on in setting up your savings program are setting your goals, paying yourself first, and sticking to a budget. Be especially vigilant, insistent, and persistent in this area, as it's the key to a debt-free education. Remember, when the summer is ending just before college, students may think they should gear up for the fall semester by slacking off in their work and spending more time shopping. This isn't the time to blow the budget because of the emotional excitement of beginning the school year.

Even if they have received a college acceptance letter and financial awards (scholarships and grants), the savings program shouldn't come to a halt. In fact, this is the time to hang tough, parents and students alike, and bank as many dollars as possible to help cover the real costs of attending college, such as tuition, fees, books, living expenses, and incidentals.

Encourage your future college graduates to save a minimum of 10 percent of everything earned before and during college, invest it, and let it grow throughout their collegiate career. In fact, insist on it. This will create a substantial reward they can gift themselves at graduation.

Needs versus Wants: Knowing the Difference

> *Give a man a fish and you feed him for a day. Teach him to fish and you feed him for a lifetime.*
> — Chinese Proverb

One of the most important lessons we can teach our children is knowing the difference between wants and needs. We must understand that we cannot buy or pay for the wants until the needs are taken care of first. Part of our job as parents is to prepare children to deal effectively with life after leaving the sanctuary of the home. If children are allowed to become dependent or accustomed to us giving them unessential things—money, cars, cell phones—as they are growing up, they may very well expect the same even after they graduate. In many cases, parents, thinking or feeling they should make life less challenging for their children, will allow themselves to go broke or deeper in debt doing so.

Many parents, me included, have given in at times when the pride of our lives, our children, have asked for something. We spare no expense and sometimes make personal sacrifices to satisfy their wants. But if this pattern is allowed to continue to satisfy their immediate gratification, we are doing them a grave injustice when it comes time to face the reality of living their own lives.

Needs are food, shelter, clothing, and companionship; everything else is a want. Of course, our wants can be endless, and if our resources are limited, we have to make good choices about which ones to fulfill. The way we fulfill our needs involves a lot of choices.

Shelter, for example, can be a basic affordable home or, to satisfy a want, a million-dollar mansion. Food choices offer a similar range, from peanut butter and jelly sandwiches at home to burgers and pizza at fast food places to going out for steak and lobster at a four-star restaurant. Clothing needs can be met at thrift or box stores, seasonal sales at department stores, or choosing to purchase top of the line merchandise at a prestigious boutique.

Companionship is also a need. However, sometimes it can come with a high price when a person is more into wants than a fulfilling life based on spiritual principles. Sometimes those wants can come with excess baggage, including debt (student loans and credit cards) coupled with the delusion of how to live the American dream.

All of our needs involve choices on how we meet those needs. Our choices should always be based on affordability, not credit terms. It takes a great deal of determination and effort to resist buying something you want on credit when you don't have cash to pay for it in full.

Too much emphasis today is on acquiring possessions by incurring debt through easy credit in order to finance an immediate want, not a need, and therefore the old interest factor comes into play. It seems many people would rather have a mountain of interest to pay back than build equity and financial stability for the future. They're choosing short-term gratification and risking long-term stress and failure.

The Friendly Hometown Banker

During some of my memorable days in construction, I had a good working relationship with my friendly hometown banker. Whenever a deal would show up, I would try to take advantage of it, whether it was land or a piece of equipment, and occasionally I would have to borrow money to buy it.

When I'd make the call to my banker and tell him what I wanted to do, he would always ask me, "Well, do you *need* it?" This question always caused me to pause a moment and ponder over the decision. Sometimes I realized I just wanted it and didn't really need it, and when I realized the difference, I wouldn't buy it.

Then there would be the time when the item was really needed for my business, and I would tell him yes. Then he'd asked how much it was, and I'd give him the price, whether it was $5,000 or $50,000. He would tell me to go ahead, make the deal, and write a check, as the check was covered. Then, when I had some time, I could come on into the bank, and they'd take care of the paperwork.

Most of the time, I only borrowed when it was necessary to finance something for my business. If it was just something I wanted, I didn't believe it was worth borrowing and going into debt over. Now if I really wanted it and had cash to buy it, that might be a different story.

Many of the people you know believe they *have* to spend money in certain ways or in certain amounts or for certain things. But spending is always a choice—even when it's based on choices made earlier. For example, a mortgage payment on that million-dollar mansion has to be made because they chose to buy that particular-priced home with that specific mortgage. Taking responsibility for your choices projects maturity and personal empowerment. It shows the world you have chosen not to be a victim of circumstance.

Part of our job as parents is to prepare our children to deal effectively with life after leaving the sanctuary of the home. If our children grow accustomed to us giving them things beyond necessities as they are growing up—such as money, cars, and cell phones—they may very well expect the same even after they graduate. In many cases, parents, thinking or feeling they should make life less challenging for their children, will allow themselves to go broke or deeper in debt doing so. To find true happiness and satisfaction in our lives, we need to look beyond our wallets.

Being a Value-Based Consumer

Teach your young person how important it is to become a value-based consumer buying quality products, when needed and planned for, at a discounted or sale price. Where is it written that you must pay retail? Encourage the buying of used items or equipment—such as textbooks, car, bicycle, or computer—that will meet needs just as well as new equipment. Estate sales and thrift shops quite often have quality items at hugely discounted prices. However, be wary of used computers, as viruses and unwanted programs may be contained within the hard drive.

Advocate and teach comparison shopping, using coupons, and asking for discounts. Avoid impulse buying by only buying items planned for in advance. We know only too well there are a million things to buy. If we allow impulse buying to influence our spending habits, then our impulses are in control and not us. We're not talking about always buying cheap products. On the contrary, a little bit more spent on a quality item (on sale) will yield long-term usability.

A very successful entrepreneur and multimillionaire always stresses value-based buying, including shopping at garage, moving, and estate sales where the savings are endless in today's throwaway society. His guiding principle is to "always buy in stores with concrete floors."

Buy a Used Car

Emphasize to your future student that a car should be paid for in cash and kept as long as possible. This puts you or your student in control of the deal and reduces the emotional factor to a more logical buying decision. Ask yourself these questions first before buying:

- What kind of vehicle should I seek that will meet my needs (not wants); get me to and from school, home, and job safely and dependably; and be chosen for its tool or utility value, not its value as a status symbol?
- What can I comfortably afford, considering the initial cost along with ability to budget for necessary ongoing maintenance (oil changes, tires, etc.) plus insurance and fuel? Think in terms of value, needs, and affordability, not of personal gratification and wants.

Buy used vehicles, preferably from a private individual, or work with an auto broker to get a good deal through an auto auction. However, be sure to insist on a mechanical and overall inspection by a trusted mechanic before signing on the dotted line. You are looking for reliability, not a drain on your budget.

Also, to get the best price, be mentally prepared to walk away from the deal and out the door. Your willingness to walk away is your best bargaining strategy, as it keeps you in control and will get you the lowest price. Don't forget to factor in campus permits, and make every effort to avoid parking fines.

Quiz Time

1. Seed money will multiply when planted in areas of

    A) Savings
    B) Investments
    C) Tithing or giving
    D) All of the above

2. It is unrealistic to expect high school or college students to balance their checkbooks.

    A) True
    B) False

3. Long-term savings habits practiced by parents and shared with their children are important in meeting the future cost of a college education.

    A) True
    B) False

4. When buying a car, the best strategy is to be in a cash position and willing to walk away if the right deal cannot be negotiated to meet your budget.

    A) True
    B) False

5. The average household today could possibly save $2,000 annually by eliminating credit card debt.

    A) True
    B) False

6. College students are responsible users of credit cards and understand the fees and the effects of compounding interest on their balances.

    A) True
    B) False

7. Knowing the difference between wants and needs is not important in the financial management of your money.

   A) True
   B) False

8. If you do not control your money habits and spending patterns, they are in control.

   A) True
   B) False

Answer: 1. D; 2. B; 3. A; 4. A; 5. A; 6. B; 7. B; 8. A

The values and principles of good money management are more important today than at any other time in the history of this country. This includes being a budgeter, a consistent saver, a value-based consumer, a judicious user of credit cards, and someone who lives within your means. It involves applying knowledge and effort in pursuing the goal of attaining a debt-free college education through working, saving, and selecting the right investments. It takes a willing mind and the desire to succeed to make it all work.

Chapter 3
Investing in Success

Investing is like planting a tree. Like an acorn, even the smallest investment holds great potential. Investing requires patience. Results don't spring up overnight.
— *James E. Stowers*

Be very clear in your goals and adhere to a sound, proven, balanced system for investing money consistently in more than one basket. As an example, if you have a 401k, balance it with certificates of deposit, savings bonds, conservative stocks, and income-producing real estate, because you have no guarantee your 401k won't go south and end up as a 101k.

Invest the time, effort and due diligence in seeking out the right investment vehicles that align with your goals. Seek those areas where your expertise, energy and passion can help to generate favorable returns. The objective is to have several streams of income outside your normal job or profession. Teach these same principles to your future college student.

We are the builders of our fortunes.
— *Ralph Waldo Emerson*

Purchase a Rental Property

One practical way of setting up a second stream of income is to purchase a single-family home, condominium, townhome, or a duplex close to the college of choice. Your student can live in and learn to manage (with assistance) the unit as well as renting rooms to other qualified students.

Let the rent, appreciation, and tax benefits pay for the college education. If you have other children who later will be attending the same college, now you have really enhanced the opportunity for a debt-free education.

If you consider this to be an option, begin by analyzing the housing market as soon as possible for location, availability, and cost of ownership versus campus housing. Not all college towns will be good investments because of overpricing, business conditions, and resale factors. However, many college communities can and do provide excellent opportunities if you do your homework. What are some of the benefits for your student?

- Your student gains an opportunity to learn business finance, management, and public relations skills.
- Your student will see an increase in net monthly income (after debt service and expenses are paid) that, supplemented with additional income from part-time work and scholarships, can take care of college expenses and lifestyle needs.
- Your student will feel the pride and responsibility of ownership.
- Your student will learn how to do certain maintenance and repair tasks that will be needed in life after college.
- The more interest, care, and involvement taken by your student with the property, the greater the focus on school, with improving grades.
- Your student will learn some great lessons about real estate investments, dealing with people, planning, marketing, and making a commitment to the community to keep property presentable.
- Your student will gain confidence in making decisions as well as learn to deal with challenging and oftentimes dirty jobs that happen with all rental properties, from making repairs to establishing relationships with plumbers, electricians, and heating and cooling contractors.
- Your student may very well find, with all these lessons acquired, that these are more valuable in preparation for work and life after college than a lot of the coursework taken.

The real gift very possibly comes after graduation, when the property is sold and your student finds out how much it has appreciated, realizing the profits will pay off the mortgage, cost of improvements, and most college expenses without a future burden of student debt. If you really want to make a difference in your student's life and provide preparation for the real world, take a leap of faith and support your student in acquiring and managing a rental property. This one you won't regret.

The Law of Mind/Action

> *You are today where your thoughts have brought you; you will be tomorrow where your thoughts take you.*
> — *Ralph Waldo Emerson*

Your thoughts, actions, and belief system have more power than you may realize. They are responsible for not only your current state or circumstances but determine your future results as well. The law of mind/action states that what you think and do comes back to you in kind. Accordingly, when you think and speak uplifting thoughts and take positive actions, then positive results will be your reward. For instance, if you work hard and smart; tithe, save, and invest; and avoid credit card and student loan debt, then a debt-free college education and a prosperous life will be the reward.

If people think and speak negative thoughts—victimizing, condescending, being critical, and taking little or no positive action—then negative results will be their reward. For instance, if their belief system consists of a poverty mentality, with thoughts and actions aligning with that mentality, they are going to be poor forever with a lifetime of debt. Again, to change one's results requires changing one's beliefs.

My dad told me a story about the president of a great railroad who was on an inspection tour when he encountered a laborer in a section gang with whom he had worked in that same job some forty years earlier. He greeted his old friend warmly, remembering the old days.

The tired old laborer said, "Bert, you've gone a long way from the time when we were laying tracks together."

The executive replied, "No, Sam, that isn't quite correct. You were laying tracks. I was building a railroad."

We always have a choice as to which path we follow. Understand, teach, and integrate these laws into everyday life. Use personal examples or experiences of these laws when practiced faithfully as well as examples of consequences when they're ignored. As one can say no to drugs, a person can also say no to the addictive nature of gambling with credit card debt. It's your choice and your challenge to continue laying tracks or building a railroad.

> *Expose yourself constantly to wealthful ideas—think prosperity, think substance, think affluence. Your life will be influenced for good or ill by the kinds of thoughts that rule your mind and manifest in your world. Spiritual Economics is all about such thoughts.* — Eric Butterworth

Tithing

As a parent, you believe in helping others by donating your time, talents, and tithes to your church or favorite charity, and by living this belief, you enroll your children into this model. You help them understand that 10 percent of everything they earn is tithed or contributed to help others. There's a spiritual law regarding giving which affirms that the more you give, the more you'll receive in kind.

L. E. Meyer wrote the following about tithing:

> Through prayer and blessing, we give special attention to the tithe and send it out to multiply and to be a blessing. By words of Truth, we free our symbols from all the limitations placed upon them by untrained minds. We can think of the tithe as a messenger sent from God to free all people who are in bondage to limitation.
>
> Tithing establishes order in our minds, bodies, and circumstances. When order exists, we cannot remain in debt. People who begin to tithe while in debt invariably report later that they are free from debt.
>
> The tithe goes to increase the thought of abundance, not to spread the thought of lack. Tithing will not make

one poorer, but richer if he or she is a faithful steward of that which is given directly to them.

Or as Albert Schweitzer put it, "I don't know what your destiny will be, but one thing I know: The only ones among you who will be really happy are those who will have sought and found how to serve." Those who are faithful in their tithing own their property; it does not own them.

The Law of Attraction

According to Earl Nightingale, "To attract that which you want, you must become that very thing." What you project out to others is what you'll attract in return. When you project a positive presence, a supportive and caring attitude, a helping hand, and a doer's mind-set, you attract those of like mind into your circle.

The Importance of Networking

Will Rogers said that, "A man learns by two things. One is reading. The other is association with smarter people." This is the foundation for everything that follows. Learning to develop and build relationships with others is essential to you and your student's success. You and I can do many things individually; however, so much more can be accomplished with the assistance of others.

Imparting this skill and commonsense approach to creating lasting relationships to your student must be a high priority. Use examples of real-life situations you've experienced which demonstrate the effectiveness of having a valued network.

How Can I Help?

The value of having a personal network was brought home to me at the end of my son's sophomore year at a major university. His attention had become fully engaged in the college experience over focusing on his studies, attending classes, or pursuing a career objective. He joined a fraternity, quit his part-time job, and took out student loans in addition to my financial help to support his lifestyle.

When my bank account began suffering, I called him to find out why, and that's when I became fully aware of his activities on campus. I was very frank with the young man, telling him I could no longer afford to pay for college. He had to make a choice. He had to drop out, get a job, or join the military. His only other choice was to get straight on what he wanted to do and be willing to commit to that. Until he did, Dad was through financing his college experience. When he decided what he wanted to do with his life, he was to call me.

Jeff called three weeks later to inform me that he wanted to go into education and become a teacher, as his mother had been before she passed away during his junior year in high school. I supported his decision and asked where he was going to pursue his degree. He said through the School of Education at Kansas University. He applied and called three weeks later, crying, saying they wouldn't accept him because of his grades. It was probably his first major rejection in life.

I asked how important it was to him to become a teacher, and he said it was very important. I then asked if he would consider going to Emporia State University. He quickly said yes, but if KU wouldn't accept him, why would Emporia State?

His mother and I had graduated from Emporia with our bachelor's and master's degrees, and afterward, I worked for the college and had many friends there. Although I left the college to run my own business, I still kept in touch with several of my contacts, including Professor Jack Skillet. Jack was a former high school principal and district superintendent who now taught school administration at Emporia. He and I fished together and soon became friends. His areas of expertise included administration, contract negotiations, investments, and fishing.

Our family had moved to Kansas City, and although we hadn't visited for several years, I knew Jack was the one to get in touch with. I called, and after a few pleasantries, I said, "Jack, I normally wouldn't ask for a favor, but there's a situation I need some help with."

Without hesitation, he replied, "Charley, how can I help?"

I explained Jeff's situation, and Jack immediately said, "You send the young man down here to see me. If he's willing to enter on a probationary status, I'll get him into the teacher education program and personally keep a watchful eye over him."

Jack was at that time the dean of the School of Education. Jeff was admitted to the program, graduated with an education degree, and was hired by the Kansas City, Kansas, school district as an English as a Second Language coordinator. Later, after obtaining his master's degree in school administration from Kansas University, he accepted an elementary principal position in the Ottawa, Kansas, school system. Recently, he was selected into a doctoral program in education at the University of Kansas. This program is fully funded by the US Department of Education. Consequently, his doctorate degree will be a debt-free investment for him.

This is only one example of the possibilities that exist through networking. However, you have got to do the homework and put forth the effort to make it happen. Keep this thought in mind. Our personal network, those we associate with, will determine our future net worth.

Emphasize to your children that everyone they meet has talents, knowledge, and experiences different from their own and may be a potential resource for help on their journey. Teach them how to create a contact list and add to it with names, business cards, addresses, phone numbers, special notes, and e-mail addresses of people they come in contact with. This will be invaluable for resources and connections in the future.

Encourage an Active Role in Student Organizations

> *Keep company with the wise and you will become wise. If you make friends with stupid people, you will be ruined.*
> — *Proverbs 13:20*

Students should be encouraged to join an organization in their major field plus one in an area of interest, all of which will lead to other resource possibilities. As your student becomes involved and aware of the value of the networking process, short-term and long-term relationships and opportunities will develop. However, over involvement in organizational and social activities may alter their focus toward their main priority for being at college. That could have an impact on their budget, studies, and work—all determining factors on whether or not they graduate as planned with a minimum of debt.

Follow-Up

It's the power of Positive Doing that makes the difference.
— Bill Gove

Model and emphasize the importance and courtesy of following up and giving thanks when your student has received assistance in some form, whether a favor, a lead, or an opportunity. A top priority is to stay in touch as often as possible with one's network without being a pest. Your student must keep the network informed of personal progress and share information of value to individuals in the network. It's a two-way street. The opportunity to create, develop, or enhance a money-generating idea or add onto an existing one increases exponentially when the energy of others is focused on your goals.

Value-Based Foundation

The freshman year is the foundation for the college experience. College is great for learning and social experiences, but it's not the place for your student to go crazy making bad choices and wind up broke and maxed out on credit cards. However, there are a certain number of money and social lessons students must learn when they begin to stretch out and have a sense of freedom on their own.

If you have constructed a good values-based foundation over the years, the college experience will be rewarding and beneficial, giving a feeling of pride and accomplishment. Occasionally, there may come a moment when your student strays off the path for a period of time. If you have done your homework, the student will come back on course. Teach the true meaning of gratitude, the value of learning, and the gift of earning.

Quiz Time

1. Finding the right investment vehicle requires

    A) Time
    B) Effort
    C) Due diligence
    D) All the above

2. Is networking a skill that can be learned and applied to the building of relationships?

   A) Yes
   B) No

3. The power of an effective personal network cannot be underestimated, nor should it be abused.

   A) True
   B) False

4. Student organizations play an important part in developing personal networking skills.

   A) True
   B) False

5. Following up with and keeping your personal network informed of your progress is not important in maintaining those relationships.

   A) True
   B) False

6. The Laws of Attraction and Mind/Action are of little importance in reaching our goals.

   A) True
   B) False

7. A student, as well as parents, must realize that everyone they meet may has

   A) Talents and resources different from their own.
   B) A network of their own to provide other connections and opportunities.
   C) A personal contact which can open other doors and provide a solution to a problem.
   D) All of the above

8. Providing a values-based environment for children growing up in the home is essential to their future success.

   A) True
   B) False

Answers: 1. D; 2. A; 3. A; 4. A; 5. B, 6. B; 7. D; 8. A.

Networking, the human connection, has always been the most effective way to achieve success in personal and financial affairs. Many things can be accomplished by the individual on their own; however, so much more can be accomplished with the help of others who can provide resources, contacts, and guidance.

It is crucial for students as well as their parents to develop the skills of effective networking in order to build long-term relationships with the right people who are supportive and in alignment with their goals. It is not a one-way street, as it requires giving and sharing as well as the receiving of information and support.

The Doing Phase

Apply for All Grants and Scholarships

> *The miracle power that elevates the few is to be found in their industry, application and perseverance, under the promptings of a brave determined spirit.*   — Mark Twain

Grants and scholarships do not have to be repaid. However, there is the responsibility to act appropriately and use the funds wisely. Timing is critical, as demand is high. The early bird has the advantage, so begin early and research diligently. This isn't an area in which to be timid, reserved, or a procrastinator. Set a goal, make a commitment, and put in the effort to apply for at least fifty scholarships.

As your efforts in this area yield results, keep in mind the plan to win goals. When the gifts, grants, and scholarship goals have been reached and exceeded, have a rule in place that states clearly that any extra or unexpected income is to be deposited in a savings or investment account. Continue to apply for grants and scholarships even after meeting your goals, as the importance of having a reserve cannot be understated. It may very well be needed later in the event an unplanned or unexpected situation occurs, either in the way of an investment opportunity or a crisis.

There's a lot of information on grant and scholarship availability as well as an application process. This is where you need to begin your work, and the following are some of the possibilities of where to look. You have got to do your own work here, so be wary of companies or individuals claiming they'll find you a scholarship for a fee.

The value of striving for above-average grade points hasn't been discussed, although it is very important in attracting quality scholarships. Mediocre grades can indicate below-average effort. Those students will probably have to settle for above-average student-loan amounts.

Insist your students apply for scholarships from professional organizations in their field of study, such as education, medical, and business associations. Additionally, contact private and/or independent foundations in your community that support education, such as the Kauffman Foundation in the Kansas City area, which sponsors a great program named the Kauffman Scholars. Research and persistence will pay off in this area.

Scholarships from Service and Fraternal Organizations

> *Great discoveries and improvements invariably involve the cooperation of many minds. I may be given credit for having blazed the trail but when I look at the subsequent developments I feel the Credit is due to others rather than to myself.* — *Alexander Graham Bell*

Apply to organizations and clubs such as the Fraternal Order of Eagles, Lions International, Rotary, Masons, Library Clubs, and many other organizations. Remember, even $100 received from these organizations adds up, so be sure to insist that your students keep these organizations informed of their progress. They can do this with a quarterly newsletter outlining their progress in college as well as making a presentation to the organization at the end of the school year.

This is a two-way street to build confidence within the student and rapport with an organization. It also keeps your student in front of the organization and makes it easier to obtain additional aid throughout the college years. Encourage your student to volunteer and be of service in whatever area the organization deems appropriate. It's not only what the organization can do for your student; it's what your student can do for them. It's a great networking possibility for job or business opportunities during school, summertime, or after graduation.

Scholarships from Local or National Businesses

Consider Chick-fil-A, McDonald's, Walmart, Burger King, UPS, etc., and evaluate the benefits to be received from the employment commitment. These can include networking, learning what makes a business successful, and knowing those lessons can be of value in life's realities.

Scholarships, Tuition Reimbursement, or Assistance from Your Employer

Have your future college graduate apply for scholarships at your company, as well as any union, professional, service, or fraternal organizations to which you belong.

Scholarships from Agricultural Businesses or Associations.

If you are in a rural community, it will pay dividends to check out the 4-H clubs; farm bureau; farm, dairy, and ranch organizations associations; as well as magazines, farm stores, and restaurants like Machine Shed. Most of these groups and federations support education in voice and deed by providing scholarships and grants. Always give value-added service. Show your gratitude and appreciation.

Work for the College, Provide Services, and Barter

Often, colleges have programs where children of employees get their tuition free or at a substantial discount. If you live in the area and want to be part of the college environment, then pursue this possibility.

Another option is to contact as high up in the administration as you can and offer your services in lieu of (trade-off) certain college expenses for your student. First, determine what you have to offer, and then learn what the school needs. You may have a service or special knowledge, such as a contracting, material supply, training, consulting, speaking, even guest lecturing in specific areas. You may be willing to do a construction project or provide an intern program for students. Also, the right college may be willing to do a little bartering of a project, equipment, services, or livestock in exchange for tuition and fees.

Let your best thinking and creativity work for you. At the same time, you will be modeling, teaching results, and showing your student there's more than one way to achieve a goal. However, students must still do their part and assume responsibility and accountability for a large part of their education.

Student Employment

Upon reentering civilian life after fulfilling my military obligation with the United States Navy, my goal was to go to college and pursue a career in business. With savings accumulated from time served, I had enough money to pay for my freshman year. To build on that, I signed on with a summer crew hired to dismantle government grain bins located in Western Kansas that were no longer needed by the federal government. These bins were scattered throughout that part of the state, which meant a lot of time on the road during the hot summer months doing hard, dirty, and oftentimes dangerous work. However, the pay was better than any work available around home, and most of those on the crew were either in college or planning on going in the fall, as I was.

It turned out to be a great opportunity for networking, even though at the time I thought I was just making friends. Many of those attending college were football players. A few were fraternity members. The rest of us would be classified as independents. Most would be attending Emporia State University in the fall.

So not only did I earn great wages, I also became acquainted with those I would be seeing on campus, which helped me adjust socially. One of those acquaintances would later become a mentor as I became involved with the Collegiate Young Republicans and the Blue Key National Leadership

Fraternity. After college, he entered the legal profession and represented me in legal matters when I became a real estate entrepreneur.

Another friend introduced me to refereeing—for pay—basketball games for grade school and junior high programs, and another paved the road at the student employment office, where many part-time and temporary jobs were directed my way. As a result of developing a "will do and can do" relationship with the student employment officials, I was hired by that department as student director in charge during my senior year.

After graduation, because of my work performance, I was recommended for and hired as an assistant director for the campus student union, where I served for the next five years, during which time I earned my master's degree while working full-time. These are just a few examples of a path that showed up for me because of signing on as a hired hand dismantling grain bins and allowing the networking process to work in my behalf.

Tuition Credits, Discounts, and Reimbursements

You have not because you ask not! —James 4:2

Teach your children to always ask for credits and discounts. For planning purposes, check with the college of choice and see if they offer a guaranteed tuition plan, which allows parents and students to know what the tuition rate would be through graduation. Not only would this help in financial planning, but it could also be an incentive for the student to complete the degree in a timely manner.

Another way to cut the cost of a college education is to "quiz out" of as many courses as possible. This will give your student course credits, thereby reducing tuition and book costs.

After high school or completion of an associate's degree, encourage your student to explore any opportunities to work for a company with a tuition-reimbursement program. Many companies have programs for their employees that pay for tuition and books. Research the companies in your area that may have such programs.

If your student has been in the work world and taken specific training, classes, or seminars, some universities will grant college-level credit for prior training and learning. For example, the University of Phoenix will give students up to thirty credits based on prior learning. They and others have specific guidelines as to what kind of training and experience earns what kind of credit, so be sure to check this out.

Many colleges offer online courses that are less expensive than "live" courses and are available twenty-four hours a day, seven days a week, with the click of a mouse. These can be taken during the school year, summer vacation, and between semesters. Many people even get a degree via online technology. Be sure the online college is fully accredited and the classes taken are accepted at the college or vocational school of choice. Additionally, a student in high school can earn college credits by taking advanced placement classes before applying for full-time enrollment.

The Military Option—a Great Way to Pay for College

This could be the best and smartest way to achieve a debt-free college education: being of service to one's country as well as acquiring long-term benefits ranging from educational to financial, home ownership, and medical. This includes financial aid and college funds to programs converting military training into college credit, providing more ways than ever before for service members to further their education during or after service.

Students can receive college credits for time in service and for any specialized training while in the military. They'll also receive substantial financial benefits for college under the Montgomery GI Bill in addition to the credits.

Another option would be to join the army reserve or army national guard while attending college and receive ongoing educational benefits throughout your career. Or enlist after graduation and take advantage of the College Loan Repayment Program. At this time, up to $20,000 for college loans can be repaid for a service commitment of six years. Another consideration would be to enlist in the regular army after graduation. Soldiers and sailors on active duty can receive up to $65,000 for college loan repayment.

Check out the ROTC programs for the army, navy and air force, as they offer tuition, books, and a monthly living allowances while in school. It's a practical and sensible way to get most of a college education paid for, as well as demonstrating to a prospective employer leadership, discipline, and goal-driven qualities and skills. Another major avenue to a paid-for college degree are the military academies, including those of the air force, army, coast guard, and navy. When you consider the education value, leadership training, discipline, and experience, what better way to prepare to handle life challenges and achieve career goals?

The rising cost of tuition can be hard to manage, but the military's tuition assistance program gives service members the opportunity to enroll in courses at accredited colleges, universities, junior colleges, and vocational-technical schools. This program pays up to 100 percent of the cost of tuition or expenses, up to a maximum of $250 per credit and a personal maximum of $4,500 per fiscal year per student.

Each service has unique programs that can help with tuition for anything from professional certifications to a graduate degree. To qualify, there are usually conditional requirements, such as having a minimum time remaining on your service contract and a cap on credit hours (or dollars) per year. This program is the same for full-time-duty members in all military services. Selected reserve and national guard units also offer tuition assistance programs, although the benefits may vary from the active duty programs.

The army and navy offer programs that help enlisted personnel pay off college loans accrued prior to service. While each program has unique processes and requirements, they're all enlistment incentives designed to help recent college graduates manage education debt.

In the full-time-duty army, soldiers can qualify to have their loans repaid by the military at the rate of one-third of the loan for each year of full-time duty served (maximum loan repayment is $65,000). The army even helps soldiers pay off student loans they've taken out, provided they attended schools on approved Perkins, Stafford, or other Department of Education guaranteed student loans. In the full-time-duty navy, a $65,000 loan repayment program is also available. Qualifications include no prior military service, a high school diploma, and a loan guaranteed under the Higher Education Act of 1965. If an individual does qualify, either of these programs is a great way to get out of debt.

This is general information and is subject to change as the needs of the military change. An important factor not to be overlooked regarding the value of fulfilling a military obligation is the personal clarity received in career and life choices that results from the experience. Most veterans attending college are very clear on what they want to do. They are able to maintain discipline in their studies and focus on achieving career goals. For those of us who served, it was a life-changing experience.

This overview should stimulate your thought processes and give you a realistic way to achieve a college degree, meet career objectives, develop leadership skills, and not break the bank. If a debt-free education is truly your goal, then go to todaysmilitary.com or talk to a recruiter to find out the branch of service that meets your needs, investigate its eligibility requirements, find out about available benefits, and ask for an application.

Other Possibilities to Investigate

Research availability of internship positions in the area of interest or study. Medical, legal, educational, or animal sciences are possibilities. Also check with any related associations and ask who of their membership has intern programs. Some intern programs will also pay a stipend for living expenses.

Seek out and ask a small, medium, or large company for sponsorship. These may be interested in employing students both during and after completion of their schooling. Most small to medium companies will tell you that good help is almost impossible to find. Strike a deal and sign an employment contract agreeing to work for them if they front tuition money. Students can work over the summer or on weekends and take the opportunity to earn while they learn.

One area not to overlook for the more vocationally minded student is the automotive, airline, or building trades industry. Most of the skilled trades, such as mechanics, collision repair technicians, carpentry, electrical, plumbing, and sheet metal, have earn-as-you-learn programs that pay beginning apprentices in training well above the minimum wage. Hourly wages, depending on the chosen craft, go up significantly as a student progresses through these three- to five-year programs. An added value is that student loans are not needed. For additional information, check with your local trade or vocational school or one of the major trade unions.

Many foreign countries are in dire need of medical or engineering graduates willing to work for them. This may be another avenue to consider. Check with the foreign language department at your college as well as any foreign embassies or trade delegations or representatives located in your community.

Quiz Time

1. In the search for grants and scholarships, it is important to

    A) Start planning early.
    B) Avoid procrastination.
    C) Keep your goal clearly in sight at all times.
    D) All of the above

2. Military service is an option in the quest for a debt-free college education.

    A) True
    B) False

3. There is no cost advantage of taking online accredited e-learning courses over a live classroom environment.

    A) True
    B) False

4. Internships and sponsorships can provide on-the-job experience and tuition assistance.

    A) True
    B) False

5. Service, fraternal, and business organizations often provide scholarship awards.

    A) True
    B) False

6. Skilled trade organizations, such as construction, automotive, and mechanical, have the least interest in providing pay-as-you-learn programs.

    A) True
    B) False

7. Which of the following support scholarships in agriculture?

   A) Farm, dairy and ranch organizations
   B) Restaurants with rural heritages
   C) Magazines serving the agricultural community
   D) All of the above

8. Students should make every effort to "quiz out" on as many courses as possible to reduce tuition, fees, and book cost.

   A) True
   B) False

Answers: 1. D; 2. A; 3. B; 4. A; 5. A; 6. B; 7. D; 8. A

There are many sources and programs available for grants and scholarships that do not carry the payback burden of student loans. With effort, tenacity, and persistence, your student should be able to secure sufficient funds to supplement working income and savings and achieve the goal of a debt-free college education.

You and your student have many opportunities to reduce tuition, fees, and book costs. However, it takes willingness and creativity to find those ways along with the courage to step up and make it so. Many parents and students would rather take the easy, loan way out rather than make the effort to go to the next level in reaching their goal.

Value of Working

> *When I was young I observed that nine out of every 10 things I did were failures, so I did 10 times more work.*
> — *George Bernard Shaw*

Sometimes, students will need to take on a job that's not their first choice; however it may be necessary at the time to prepare them for later success.

Down and Dirty Pays

I once asked a client how he went through college and whether he chose the loan route or the debt-free approach. He said his goal was to always to have money in his pockets, and the strategy was to pay for his education with cash. He had his father to thank for this philosophy and determination. He always looked for and took those jobs that paid the most money. These jobs were usually the hardest, the dirtiest, and the ones most students wouldn't do.

However, not only did those jobs pay for his education, they taught him discipline and persistence. Plus, it gave him an understanding of, appreciation of, and ability to work with men and women who do this kind of work. He added that one of the biggest lessons he gained was that those jobs were not going to be part of his career path after college. However, those jobs taught him how to work with people, the importance of financial management, and an awareness of effective work processes and systems—lessons that proved to be important in his successful career.

This gentleman rose to be CEO of a major international corporation and attributed a great part of his success to the learning and practicing of financial management in his personal life. He believed this was a key in being able to effectively manage an extremely profitable multimillion-dollar company. By the way, his long-range plan after retirement was to own and operate a vineyard and winery in the wine country of California. He credits the frugality, lessons, and values learned from doing those early jobs, as well as the lessons and benefits gained from the business world, for allowing him to realize his dream: the Six Sigma Ranch in Lower Lake, California.

As a side note, check out the Six Sigma business model, processes, and techniques and see if it has an application and value in the journey to acquiring a debt-free college education. Those who become knowledgeable and skilled in this program earn higher than average incomes.

Teach future graduates to be paid well for their best thinking and to give quality service in their efforts. Very few people think through the important concepts or principles impacting their future. Be the one who does, and be open to new and out-of-the box ideas. Every successful business and individual from various professions employs this type of thinking.

> *You cannot help men permanently by doing for them what they could and should be doing for themselves.*
> — *Abraham Lincoln*

Earning Their Way

> *Every day I get up and look through the Forbes list of the richest people in America, if I'm not there, I go to work.*
> — Robert Orben

Your student should plan on working at least twenty hours a week during school to meet the planning-to-win goals on working. This should provide enough money for basic needs, if students adhere to the money principles. Assist them in evaluating each job and encourage them to select specific areas that provide an additional benefit beyond money, such as knowledge, food, clothing, and opportunities. Not only will these students be earning extra money, they'll be getting valuable skills, directly or indirectly helping to prepare them for their career and life after college.

The first job I had my freshman year of college didn't pay a dime in wages, but it paid off handsomely during my college career. What it did provide was lunch and dinner during the week; lunch on Saturdays; and the opportunity for a little social networking. I became a houseboy along with three other guys for a sorority located just off campus. Two of us were former servicemen, and the other two were beginning their junior year in college.

Duties included serving lunch and dinner to the members of the sorority in a formal dining-room setting. The meals were presided over by the housemother who, at the beginning of each semester, instructed the houseboys in proper table setup; correct serving procedures; and the appropriate conduct and dress for servers in a formal dining room setting. She was there as a positive influence to teach the girls proper dining-room etiquette, conduct expected of them, and the manners befitting young ladies preparing for social situations outside of the college environment.

The work took about an hour and a half for each meal, including setup and cleanup. Our meals, taken in the kitchen, were the same as the girls', and the cook made sure we didn't go hungry. This left time in the afternoons for part-time work and the evenings for studying and other activities. The work was an educational experience for us, because we were able to see a part of campus life not available to many students. By the way, I've never forgotten how to properly set a dinner table.

I did this for the first two years of college before other opportunities presented themselves. Needless to say, because of this work as a houseboy, none of us went hungry or charged meals to a credit card. We developed an informal social fraternity of our own, which brought us a certain amount of personal recognition on campus.

> *The highest reward for a person's toil is not what they get for it, but what they become by it.* — John Ruskin

Using Special Skills

Each of us has a special skill or knowledge we can teach someone else. We may not acknowledge it, but it's there. A skill set can be enhanced by helping others in some specific area, whether it's outside the classroom, in the home, in the outdoors, etc. Look for it within, and then profit from that skill to meet an unfulfilled need. These skills could include giving music lessons or tutoring other students in math, English, or any other field of endeavor.

As our world has become smaller because of technology and the immigration of foreign-language-speaking people, the need for the teaching of reading, listening, and speaking skills has increased tremendously. If students have a proficiency in another language, encourage them to consider hiring out to companies, schools, or local, state, and national governments to train and teach language skills.

Look for companies who translate English into other languages through books, audio, and video venues. Marketing, translation, and interpretation companies are great sources. Check with their foreign language departments for leads, referrals, and programs available.

If students are into writing and research, they could find work in this area for any number of businesses or groups. Graduate students usually have a master's thesis or doctoral dissertation in their future, and research for businesses or other groups may provide skills to help them produce an effective dissertation. Many organizations don't have the staff or time available to do major research, even though it's needed to support their work or project. Determine the fears, wants, and needs, then provide a solution.

Food Service Opportunities

Students could consider work as a server in a restaurant where various organizations meet and let the quality of service be their introduction. Most organizations (and possibility the food-service establishment where they work) have scholarships or financial assistance available and are always looking for applicants who are working at improving themselves through education. Follow the same concept with other customers. Your student may be surprised at who shows up to help with ideas and ways to achieve a goal. The universe will work for them if they will let it. People like to do business with and help those they know are making an effort to achieve their goals with quality service.

A friend of mine, Dave, had a very successful career as a meteorologist with a major airline and began investing in farmland before his retirement. He came from a farming background, was taught to respect the land, and after retirement, with good farming practices, developed a very successful business. However, because of failing health, he was unable to get out on his own and do the things most of us take for granted. Many times I would take him to see his farms, and occasionally I would run errands for him. Afterward, we would go to his favorite restaurant for breakfast.

Dave could be a bit of a grouch, and consequently, when eating out, certain servers would trade off with another server so they wouldn't have to wait on him—even though he was a fair tipper, especially when the service was good. One young lady, Shannon, took a liking to Dave and never hesitated to be of service when he came in, even after his health began to fail and he needed the assistance of a walker and oxygen. She was friendly, patient, and above all willing to listen to his stories and appreciate his sense of humor.

One particular morning, as Shannon was waiting on us, Dave asked her what she was doing with her life besides being a waitress. She told him it was her dream to be a nurse, and she had taken the first steps by enrolling in nursing school. However, after the first few classes, the cost was more than she'd anticipated, and she was dropping out of school.

Dave listened and then said, "Shannon, this country needs good nurses. Don't give up on your dream. There is always a way if you are willing to try."

She explained how she was on her own and occasionally worked double shifts to make enough money to pay her bills and still set some aside for school. He replied, "I know you work hard and you like people, and I want to help. When I come in next time, tell me what you need, and we'll figure out a way to make it work."

As we were leaving, I took Shannon aside and told her Dave was serious about helping her. I told her to put an estimate together of what she had done so far and how much she thought it would take financially to finish, and be ready to talk with Dave about it as soon as possible. Meantime, I would contact my resources and see what I could do to help. I assured her that with the three of us working together, her dream would be realized.

With our help and her committed efforts, Shannon completed her schooling and became a nurse. Consciously or unconsciously, she had allowed the Law of Attraction to work on her behalf by attracting into her presence someone who was willing to help. When the dream and the effort align for the right reasons, the universe provides a way. Sometimes that way is serving with compassion someone in a restaurant having breakfast.

For people- and service-oriented students, consider working at a well-known or prestigious food-service establishment. Their clients prefer above-average service and will give better-than-average tips. The same networking opportunities (and scholarship possibilities) are available here, and again, students never know who may show up at their table and help them with ways to achieve their goals. Create and nurture a great service relationship first, and the rest will unfold at the right time. Great service always receives great rewards.

Earning and Learning

Instead of your student going on the typical spring break and spending anywhere from $1,000 to $2,000, discuss the opportunity to spend time earning and learning. Another possibility is volunteer work with Habitat for Humanity, learning construction skills, or participating with a faith-based organization doing missionary work, helping those less fortunate. You'll be surprised at the skills and contacts developed, which will have an impact on their future. Don't be surprised if they're ahead of you and have already done their homework.

Summer Jobs

Do not despise the bottom rungs in the ascent to greatness.
— *Publilius Syrus*

Summer is when students can earn and save a substantial amount of money, provided they have their goals and priorities in order. Their focused efforts toward earning and saving during the summer months can go a long way toward fulfilling their part of their college obligation. This is also an important step in their maturity process as they begin assuming more decision-making and financial responsibility for their own obligations.

Strongly encourage your student to go for the kinds of jobs that pay overtime, such as those in the highway, residential, commercial, and industrial construction areas. Long hours with overtime will generate a good college fund provided they save, save, save.

Entrepreneurial Opportunities

You must understand what it is you do better than anybody else and mercilessly focus your efforts on it. — *Andy Grove*

It's important to pay attention and recognize those skills and areas of interest your student excels in, as that just may help create a way to pay for a college education. If your student has developed (with your help) the discipline of being a good worker, a self-starter, and a person who makes good choices and decisions, then an entrepreneurial venture may be profitable. It will provide some great lessons about life, prepare students to better assess career choices, and possibly pay their way through college.

No man becomes rich unless he enriches others.
— *Andrew Carnegie*

Encourage your student to develop products or services that will generate cash income. First, do research and homework to determine what type of services or information other students, individuals, and companies need and would be willing to pay for. It has to be something with low startup cost, preferably one that will create a stream of residual income during the term of the college career and possibly afterward. Starting a venture on a shoestring budget will force your student to be smarter and more careful with the way money is spent. A critical factor is putting the effort into good marketing and not wishful thinking.

Create an Investment Fund

This is an opportunity to make money work for you and your student. It is a fund to be used when an opportunity presents itself, such as purchasing and then reselling an item when another student may need to sell it quickly at a fire-sale price. Consider only those items that can be bought and resold at a substantial profit, such as musical equipment, bicycles, cars, CD/DVD players, sports equipment or appliances. Don't forget eBay and other internet opportunities available for marketing. Put the profits back into the investment fund and allow it to grow to do other deals.

Advise your student not to feel guilty about buying an item at a fire-sale price, as the owner would have sold or hocked it anyway. The seller has asked for help, and your student was available and able to assist and meet a need. A good business can be developed from this as word gets around about your willingness and ability to buy. Buy low, resell higher, and remember, you never go broke taking a profit.

It's Party Time

Remember, nothing happens until something sells. Consider doing special parties with products other students want or need. This could be cosmetics, jewelry, specialty, and unique items, all involving sales and referrals with the potential to duplicate the event over and over.

Dormitory, sorority or fraternity gift parties are possibilities. Look for and listen to what others want and then be the provider at a fee. This is also a great networking opportunity for future relationships and business. Again, timidity is not a virtue.

Business Services

Develop your network, find a need, and provide a profitable solution. Consider areas like window-washing, handyman services, house painting, delivery services, or anywhere a need is present but not being fulfilled. Confer and discuss with your student what skills, talents, and information they have (or can acquire) that will benefit someone in such a way they can be rewarded for providing it.

Lawn Care and Related Services

More and more homeowners, apartment owners, and small businesses with lawns and landscaping are using outside contractors or entrepreneurs for lawn care and services. Future graduates who like the outdoors can, with a little initiative and a small investment, build a substantial, profitable small business and grow it each year.

Add snow removal and handyman services to the business. Don't be surprised when your student has too much business handle alone and has to hire other students to help. Money management is extremely important, as well as follow-up and paying attention to details.

Vending-Machine Routes

Purchase an existing route with multiple locations at a substantial discount. Many who start up or establish a route become discouraged when they find out it's not a get-rich-quick scheme. These can be very profitable as long as one does the service and follow-up and always looks for new locations to add to the existing route. A flexible schedule for servicing is a plus in this business.

This is a highly replicable business, and reinvestment into this venture will yield good results. However, do the homework on this and do not be led into purchasing new equipment from a company with a great sales pitch promising high returns. The primary objective of these companies is to sell machines and not insure or guarantee your financial success.

By the time your student completes college, the profits and sale price should more than pay for the education. However, gather as much information as possible before committing to this business. One such place to begin is www.vendingconnection.com. Remember, it's the service given that determines the level of financial success achieved.

Dormitory Services

Look for areas of need that are not being met through regular channels. What services, for a fee, can be provided to fulfill the needs or wants of the residents? Could it be cleaning services or computer operations? Could it be researching, typing, proofreading, assistance with assignments or papers, specialized food-service provider, or the kind of tasks others don't like doing and would be willing to pay someone to do for them? Find what works and duplicate it, over and over.

Transportation Needs

Are there transportation needs from houses, dormitories, fraternities, or sororities that can be met with bicycles? If so, buy two or more used bikes and rent them out on a weekly or monthly basis. Deposit is required, and any damages should be paid for by the renter.

The importance of a personal network comes into play for marketing the service as well as leads for good used bicycles for sale. Always buy at below market value, as there may be some repairs required, and the better the deal, the better the return on your investment. Don't hesitate to walk away from a deal that doesn't meet your criteria for a positive cash situation.

Farm/Ranch Opportunities

Make an agreement with your student to farm a plot of ground (ten to thirty acres). The profits from those crops are to be used for college expenses. Set aside enough money from the profits to be used for the next year's crop. Use the same idea with livestock.

Research the markets and focus on the one or two with the greatest financial return for your efforts. Match potential with opportunity. Don't always do what has always been done.

Make a Deal with an Author

Consider buying self-help books and products at a discount (40 to 50 percent) and resell them to other students, parents, service organizations, businesses, financial aid offices, and high schools. These would be specialized books or booklets that meet a specific need in a niche market. Include seminars that appeal to the need. This would be a great opportunity for the sales-inspired student. As an example, consider this book and other products from the author.

The Internet

The internet is changing rapidly with new devices, services, and delivery methods, and if your student is on top of this, there might be an opportunity. Be creative and develop a website with a marketable product or service others would want. Think about what friends, family, and acquaintances search for on the internet, even though it may be considered frivolous or off-the-wall.

Set up the process so customers can purchase the items through e-downloads, and if it's to be shipped, be sure to include sufficient shipping and handling charges. Don't get fancy with website design; include only enough information, including the ordering process, to cause the customer to reach for a credit card.

Design the website to bring in money through value-added sales and not to impress people with bells, whistles, and fluff. Imagination, creativity, and willingness to seize a marketing opportunity is the mark of an entrepreneur. Be reputable and believable, and give a value-added service or product in return. It's important not to project an attitude of wanting something for nothing without giving something in return. Always come from integrity.

Utilize Computer Skills

Students who are adept at computers and software programs can help other individuals to set up their computers and contract for ongoing management. Don't overlook the senior citizens market, as more and more are coming online and could use assistance in setting up, as well as training in operating their computers. Tap into the senior network, and word will spread quickly.

Small businesses often need temporary help during high-volume times and holidays, and a computer-skilled person could get a job at an attractive wage. Competent computer help can earn double the minimum wage or more with a corresponding benefit to the college savings account. Print up inexpensive business cards and start putting the word around about availability and qualifications in this area. When working for and networking with clients, ask for referrals, as quality service will keep you busy and in the chips. Be of service and honor your commitments.

Become a Self-Promoter

> *I'm not here just to make a living, I'm here to make a difference.* — Helice Bridges

Encourage students to use specific expertise or acquire it so they can do the following:

- Consult with others and be paid for it.
- Write articles and booklets.
- Do radio interviews on areas of interest where a perceived need exists.
- Create functions and events.
- Do seminars on their expertise and sell related products.

Your student will learn to "show up, stand up, and speak up," or "let your message show, let it shine, and let it *sell*."

Out of Necessity Came a Vision

> *Luck is a dividend of sweat. The more you sweat; the luckier you get.* — Ray Kroc

Many students who have taken the entrepreneurial route to pay for their college education wound up creating new careers. The success of those students after college is directly attributable to their own initiative, willingness to see the possibilities, and ability to take action and make their own businesses a stream of income to finance their education.

It's also possible a multimillion-dollar business may be created out of an interest and skill in a particular area where quality service is in short supply. In the following instance, it came about because a student wanted and needed to earn enough money to pay his way through college.

Lirel Holt is quite the visionary, entrepreneur, and self-promoter. He's walking proof of what can happen when you have a dream, brand it, and then bring it into realization on a major scale. About sixteen years ago, he blended his training and seminar business into a company he started that would consolidate and standardize the auto body industry.

Lirel worked his way through college fixing cars, and after graduating, he pursued his interest by opening his first automotive collision repair business. Over a period of time, he created a better, more consistent, and more profitable system than what others were using in the industry.

Most of those in the collision repair business at the time (as well as the general public) referred to their places as *body shops*. In many cases, the owners were unprofessional, and their customers, the general public, and the insurance companies didn't hold the industry in the highest regard. There were few standards, and Lirel saw the need to incorporate systems, offering customer service training and consulting services. This was a critical step in helping his industry upgrade and position itself in the marketplace as professionally owned and operated businesses.

He then developed a franchise concept, incorporating standards of practice and operation for those who wanted to create a better image, a brand name, profitability, and greater acceptance by the public of their individual businesses and the industry. The rest is history, as CARSTAR, Inc. became the largest automotive collision repair group in the world.

As franchisor and owner of hundreds of shops, Lirel put an emphasis on branding, professionalism, and systems. He referred to his shops as stores and eventually collision repair centers. All across the country and Canada, auto body shops joined the CARSTAR family and evolved into professionally operated collision repair centers.

Can one person with a dream, goals, and persistence make a difference in an area of interest? You bet, and Lirel changed the way collision repair centers operate. And this happened because he used talents and interests to finance his way through college. So don't discourage your students' initiative or overlook the possibility of them pursuing an entrepreneurial venture.

> PRESS ON. Nothing in the world can take the place of persistence. Talent will not; nothing in the world is more common than unsuccessful men with talent. Genius will not; unrewarded genius is almost a proverb. Education will not; the world is full of educated derelicts. Persistence and determination alone are omnipotent. — Calvin Coolidge

Start a Janitorial or House-Cleaning Service

When you do the things most people dislike doing, they'll gladly pay a quality price for quality service to perform that task for them. Working times are more flexible, and you'll grow as fast or as big as you desire. Start small, invest the minimum, and envision big. Always keep your eye and focus pointed in the direction of the goal. Presentation counts. However, it's integrity and quality service that pays.

An acquaintance of mine worked his way through college in janitorial services. I asked him what drew him to this work.

He told me, "When I started college, I needed a job, and a friend referred me to a custodial service cleaning commercial buildings. There was hesitation on my part, and I told my friend I didn't think this work was for me, as I was looking for something with a better future than cleaning toilets and floors. Then my friend said something to me I've never forgotten: 'How do you know God hasn't presented you with this opportunity as He wants you to learn how to become the best janitor you can be, and in so doing, He's preparing you to develop and own the best, the largest, and the most profitable cleaning service company in this city or even the state?'"

That statement resonated with my acquaintance, so he took the job, and by his junior year in college, had started his own one-man company. By his senior year, he had fifteen employees. His college education was paid for through the janitorial service, and now he has the largest and most successful company of this type in his state. He's added subsidiary companies selling supplies and equipment as well as leasing equipment to similar businesses. Additionally, he invested his earnings in his business and real estate and has achieved a level of financial status most of us only dream about. The goal is to go through college effortlessly, debt-free, and profiting from the experience.

Bookkeeping for Independent Businesspeople

If your student is numbers-oriented and likes doing detail work, many entrepreneurs are so busy doing the business, they lack the ability or time to do some of the important functions, such as record-keeping and office organization. Bookkeeping and data entry would help them immensely, and they'll pay for this service, especially if it's part-time as a subcontractor so they won't have the payroll taxes to worry about.

Personal Expertise/Talent

> *We are what we repeatedly do. Excellence then, is not an act, but a habit.* — *Aristotle*

Special expertise in certain activities—such as computers, bodybuilding, aerobics, football, track, cheerleading, acting, modeling, and painting—can be profitable. Can your student teach others who may need those particular skills? If so, encourage your student to put on special seminars, conduct weekend camps, and do personal consulting (fee-based) for individuals or groups.

Possibly your future graduate is interested in athletics. A great way to profit is officiating sports, such as basketball, football, soccer, baseball, and softball. This is a great opportunity to work with elementary and high school students and get paid for doing so. Beginning in the freshman year, your student should work to establish credentials, gain experience, and build credibility. By the junior year of college, your student should have more work coming in than there's time for. For more information, contact your state high school activities or athletic association.

If a particular activity, one that'll pay, speaks passionately to your student, then provide support in the learning, preparation, and action to go for it.

A graduate student acquaintance who enjoys art and painting had only painted for the creative expression and her personal enjoyment. She didn't feel her paintings were good enough to put a price on. Then she had a personal revelation that got her out of her shell and in the money.

It was all about sharing the excellence of her work with others, which she reluctantly did at an art show. The day she found out she could sell her paintings for money was the day she quit painting just for the fun of it. She realized she had a talent and a vision of what folks wanted from her paintings, and the more she gave them, the more she got what she wanted: a debt-free college education. She worked at doing what she did best, and the excellence thing just fell into place. The proof is in the bank, and she still loves what she does.

She brought her talents and excellence to a particular market that was willing to pay handsomely for her paintings. So support your students in those areas where they demonstrate a marketable skill or talent. Encourage them to use those talents in developing ideas that will work in the commercial world.

Quiz Time

1. A realistic number of hours a student should work, per week, while attending college is

    A) Five
    B) Ten
    C) Twenty
    D) None of the above

2. Are there jobs available where a student can make better than the minimum wage?

    A) Yes
    B) No

3. The benefits to be gained from working include

    A) Personal networking
    B) Job skills
    C) Possible future opportunities
    D) All of the above

4. Can working for quality restaurants open doors to opportunity, scholarships, and top pay?

   A) Yes
   B) No

5. The essential attributes to being a successful entrepreneur are

   A) Good work ethics
   B) Self-starter
   C) Making good choices in creating a product that meets the needs of a specific market niche
   D) All of the above

6. A successful entrepreneur does not have to become a selfless self-promoter of his business and products.

   A) True
   B) False

7. Often, a service opportunity presents itself in a specific market that an alert and assertive parent or student can take advantage of, thereby creating a business to provide a service to those who are unwilling or unable to do certain things for themselves.

   A) True
   B) False

Answers: 1. C; 2. A; 3. D; 4. A; 5. D; 6. B; 7. A.

The One Great Possibility

The examples I presented are not the total of all possibilities. However, these ideas should help guide and stimulate your thinking to create ways of learning and modeling that will be profitable, keep everyone on point, and keep you out of debt. One or two of these may trigger your thinking in a specific area and generate a fantastic, educational, and financially rewarding idea. Find the one great possibility, enhance it, use it in combination with others, and be the proud parent whose modeling, teaching, and encouragement provided a way for your student to go through college debt-free.

There is no lazy man's way to a debt-free college education without incurring the burden of student loans which must be repaid, with interest, after graduation. There are many ways for students to earn extra money to meet their end of the bargain. However, finding the highest-paying jobs requires persistence, creativity, and the willingness to go the extra mile. Every job has a benefit in the way of experience, networking, and money earned.

Many students have taken the entrepreneurial route to paying for their college education. The success of those students after college is directly attributable to their own initiative, willingness to see the possibilities, and ability to take action to make their own businesses a stream of income to finance their education. If sending your future college graduate through college debt-free is a heartfelt desire, a willing commitment, and a pragmatic financial goal, then plan and continue to seek out and learn the best ways to embrace the principles described in this book. By practicing them as a family, you'll experience the pleasure of seeing your, and consequently your student's, financial life change for the better.

You may be surprised at the reaction of other parents and friends as you model these principles. They may even ask for your help in assisting them in overcoming the attitudes and practices they have toward money. This could even be a source of income through consulting fees. What you learn and gain, pay forward for others to profit by.

You must take a positive step toward your goal on a daily basis, so there is no room for procrastination, avoidance, and fear to creep in. These dream destroyers reduce your ability to complete the goal and increase the chances of a burden of debt. Remember: day in and day out, through the good times and tough times, the greatest lesson you can give your kids is to believe that anything is possible. Their potential for future success increases exponentially when they learn, embrace, and incorporate financial education and practices along with self-reliance. Watching their parents manifest goals and dreams will teach them more about living a successful, debt-free life than any academic program or college in the country.

This is a start, and I know great ideas and doable projects will unfold for you. Let me know of your successes and any new ideas generated as a result of this book. I especially want to hear about other creative ideas or programs you successfully pursued, and I'll include them in the next updated edition. A special few of you will embrace and put into action these ideas and principles. However, the majority will allow their future student to take the easy, burdensome loan way out. Which group will you be in?

Quiz Time

The following questions may reflect on your ability to teach kids facts about money. Be honest with yourself. The first eight you'll have to answer for yourself; for the remainder, you'll find the correct answers at the end.

1. Am I a good money manager?

   A) Yes
   B) No

2. Am I willing to share with and teach my son or daughter the realities of cash and debt management?

   A) Yes
   B) No

3. Am I comfortable talking with my children about money?

   A) Yes
   B) No

4. Do I involve my kids when paying household bills so they understand the process of bill-paying in relation to earned income—the paycheck?

   A) Yes
   B) No

5. Do I share the money mistakes made and the lessons learned from those mistakes?

   A) Yes
   B) No

6. Am I a good financial role model my kids can emulate, learn from, and then use to put into practice a sound approach to money?

   A) Yes
   B) No

7. What messages am I sending to my kids about the value of money, savings, and credit card usage?

   _____
   _____

8. Do I talk, practice, and advocate financial self-reliance and financial competency to my children?

   A) Yes
   B) No

9. Is life a business?

   A) Yes
   B) No

10. In addition to parents and the public schools, financial institutions should provide

    A) Realistic coaching in financial management
    B) Special financial education workshops, not loan-based
    C) Incentives to help make a difference in developing financially responsible adults
    D) All of the above

11. Believing that a debt-free college education is possible is the first step to achieving it.

    A) True
    B) False

12. Certain aspects of life require a businesslike approach to achieve financial success.

    A) True
    B) False

13. Budgeting is one area most people avoid in money matters.

    A) True
    B) False

14. Factors affecting the choice of colleges should include

    A) Status
    B) Prestige
    C) Parents' preferences
    D) None of the above

15. The selection of a college should consider the following:

    A) Affordability
    B) The quality of education offered
    C) The needs of the student
    D) All of the above

16. Which of the following is very important in achieving a debt-free college education and building a solid financial foundation?

    A) Saving
    B) Budgeting
    C) Income and debt management
    D) All of the above

Answers: 9. A; 10. D; 11. A; 12. A; 13. A; 14. D; 15. D; 16. D.

Call to Action

Real-life financial teaching models are not, as of yet, a required part of most elementary and secondary schools' educational curriculum. The need for adding a real-life financial program to the curriculum is beginning to be seriously considered by some school systems and state educational agencies. We must all support and encourage this trend—and take a hands-on role in bringing this to reality. The earlier the better! As Alan Greenspan has said, "In many respects, improving financial education at the elementary and secondary school level is essential to providing a foundation for financial literacy that can help prevent younger people from making poor financial decisions that can take years to overcome."

In addition to messages to you and your student, I have a list of actions you should be insisting on from those who educate your student and those who supervise those educators:

- Require and incorporate realistic financial education models in grades K-12 and college.
- Teach students one of the realities of life: the importance of being financially literate.
- Teach self-reliant strategies that will help students achieve a college education and success in life.
- Advocate as well as model effective money practices and behaviors using the best resources available.
- Find ways to help children and students develop critical thinking skills to better evaluate options and choices available.
- Use financial models in determining the true cost of college along with the value and benefits of financial education.
- Plan ways to make the investments needed and avoid unnecessary student-loan and credit card debt.

How students think and act toward their responsibilities, as well as learn to make good choices in the pursuit of their goals, will determine their degree of success in life. Your part in this development process can be enhanced by taking a realistic attitude and approach to financial matters, being consistent in applying value-based buying habits, and upholding a commitment to achieving a debt-free education. All of this becomes a powerful model for children to see and emulate.

Chapter 4
Grandparents: The Golden Years

Are you a grandparent facing retirement along with family issues concerning today's high cost of a college education? If so, this section is intended to provide awareness of, information about, and insight into a potentially challenging situation that may come knocking at your door. A factor that must be considered up front, and most grandparents are aware of this, is that senior citizens in America are delaying retirement, not necessarily because they want to, but because they don't have enough money to retire. Consequently, many seniors plan to work longer at either part- or full-time jobs.

Did you know there are approximately 40.5 million retired workers, with 90 percent, or 36.45 million, dependent on Social Security to help meet their month-to-month living expenses? Almost 60 percent, 22 million, count on Social Security benefits as a major portion of their income. The average monthly Social Security benefit just isn't enough anymore. For 2018, it will be $1,404, including a 2 percent cost-of-living increase, for an annual income of just $16,848.

Rising costs of prescription drugs, surgical procedures, and food are outpacing increases in Social Security. As of this writing, there appears to be no easing in the foreseeable future because of built-in advantages within our health care system favoring the pharmaceutical and medical industry. Retirees must also consider the uncertainty of today's economic and political climate. In 2016, there was no significant increase (0–0.01 percent) in Social Security benefits paid to beneficiaries. Although the government has projected a 2.5 percent average increase in benefits over the next ten years, we all know nothing is guaranteed. Wise retirees won't count on those projections and will make plans for a life without any increases in their benefits.

Along with prudent financial planning, emotional family issues come into play. If there is a grandchild or grandchildren approaching college age or currently in pursuit of a higher education, the possibility exists that, at some point, the grandparents will be asked to assist in paying for part of that education by cosigning a student loan. Often, this is the moment where love and guilt cross paths. Grandparents love their grandchildren, want the best for them, and hope to avoid the burden of guilt or loss of love by giving in even against their better judgment.

Unplanned situations could arise relating to financial and health issues, placing a damper on grandparents' lifestyle. This could very well be challenging in the golden years, those times when one had planned to enjoy the benefits of years of hard work and sacrifice. It is important you understand the critical long-term issues associated with debt from student loans before cosigning on the dotted line. This debt, if used indiscriminately, can have serious financial consequences for the grandparent as well as the student.

There's a myth that's been sold by the federal government, universities, and financial institutions that the only way to achieve the American dream is with a college education. This has led many grandparents, out of love for their grandkids, to believe that taking on student loans is a small price to pay for a future built on a four-year degree. Unfortunately, student loans do not come with guarantees. In too many cases, debt disaster lies in wait for those failing to exercise due diligence when signing up for student loans. This can be devastating. The American dream of generations past, and the middle-class lifestyle and financial security that it brought, will fade in the shadow of misleading information, false hopes, and unrealistic expectations.

The in-depth information presented here will help guide grandparents' decision-making process as they choose the right course of action for their and their grandkids' long-term success. The goal is for grandparents to remain self-reliant, financially solvent, and a pillar of wisdom their grandchildren can love and respect.

Again, the Ugly

How ugly? Two million Americans sixty years of age or older owe $43 billion in student loans. More than 10 percent of those loans are ninety days delinquent, and almost 25 percent are in default. This means that the feds are coming after their Social Security.

According to government data, the federal government is withholding money from a rapidly growing number of Social Security recipients who have defaulted on federal student loans. This came about with the passing of the 1991 Higher Education Technical Amendments Act, which removed time limits on the government's ability to collect from those defaulting, and the Debt Collection Improvement Act of 1996, which empowered the federal government to offset Social Security payments of defaulted student-loan borrowers. In the case of defaults, the lenders and feds are coming after the cosigner, extracting payments and fees not only from their Social Security or disability benefits but potentially from their income tax returns and estates.

The amount the government withholds can vary up to 15 percent. The average monthly Social Security benefit for a retired worker is a little more than $1,200, which could mean a monthly shortage of about $180. This could be a significant amount if every penny is needed to meet daily living expenses.

In light of the above information, it is extremely important, and cannot be overemphasized, that grandparents and parents understand that student loans are the worst kind of debt to have because they are treated differently than any other consumer or federal loan instrument in the nation's history. All other federal loan guarantees, secured or unsecured, are entitled to bankruptcy protection should circumstances dictate. Loans such as FHA, FEMA, SBA, DOE 1705 (Solyndra), and others—not a single one is exempted from bankruptcy discharge. Only student loans.

The collection processes legally granted to lenders by the federal government for past-due and delinquent student loans are without recourse. Bankruptcy or default protection in most cases are not available to the borrower. And here's the kicker, and it must be understood clearly: those same collection processes apply to the cosigner of those loans if the original borrower defaults. This could include parents or grandparents.

To reiterate, Congress granted the loan industry unbelievable methods for recovery of the increased debt, which include wage, Social Security, and disability garnishments and tax seizure. These laws and regulations have created a huge cash cow, or profit center, for the federal government, private lenders, and higher educational institutions. This legislation with its ever-increasing regulation, came about as a result of intense lobbying by financial institutions seeking loan guarantees from the federal government. Now those lenders can grant loans to high-risk borrowers and not suffer any financial consequences should the debtor default.

The lender can't lose, as it has a money-back guarantee from the government. However, students have no guarantee they will receive a quality education—or a middle-class income with the ability to repay the loans when due.

Consequences

Thousands of retirees are behind on student loans they cosigned for those they trusted—sons, daughters, or grandkids—who have since defaulted on their commitment. These retirees are learning that defaulting on student loans can threaten something that used to be untouchable: their Social Security and other benefits. The question grandparents must ask themselves before signing on the dotted line is, "In the event the unthinkable happens—default by my grandchild for whatever reason, five or ten years from now—will I be able to financially pay off that loan as a cosigner?"

This of course assumes that their health and financial status remains good. Plus, keep in mind, if the federal government decides to reduce Social Security benefits in the future, this could potentially add to and impact the overall financial woes faced by grandparents. So before you cosign, ask yourself this question: "Will I be financially able to make the payments, which may range from $500 to $1,200 per month, for the next ten to twenty years?"

Grandparents, Be Aware!

Should there be an outstanding loan balance due upon the unfortunate or unexpected death or disability of a student borrower, any cosigner will receive the fateful notice to pay off the loan balance—not only the balance outstanding but any and all fees, interest accrued, and in a worst-case scenario, liens levied on one's estate.

I have said this earlier, but it needs repeating: to protect the cosigner from a potential financial nightmare in the event death or disability occurs, insurance coverage must be in place. It's a matter of practical, realistic financial planning that a cosigner require the borrower to have insurance coverage (term or permanent whole life) as well as disability (to cover temporary income disruption disabilities, such as illness or injury) in place. The amount of coverage should be at least double the amount of total loans and name the cosigner as beneficiary. If the student borrower has money management issues, the cosigner should take out the insurance, making sure the premiums are paid when due.

Chapter 5
Students: College and Career Success

The following are ten excuses college students give to justify student loans and credit card debt:

1. After four years, I'll be able to find a good job to pay off those loans.
2. It beats working!
3. I can concentrate on my studies and especially my social life.
4. If my friends, who don't have to work, see me working, I'll probably have to find new friends.
5. I can always move back home with my parents if I can't find a job to pay for my debts and lifestyle.
6. Loans and credit card debt don't scare me none. My parents are doing okay and seem to be managing their debt without any problems.
7. My science professor says the human brain doesn't become fully developed and capable of making mature decisions until age twenty-five. When I'm twenty-five years old, then I'll make responsible decisions for my financial life.
8. Working keeps me from having the total college experience, i.e., extracurricular activities.
9. Having to work interferes with my organizational involvement. I feel developing social skills and contacts are more important than dealing with money issues.
10. Hey! My parents have always bailed me out whenever I got in trouble, so why worry?

A Dose of the Truth

One time I was taking a client from the airport to a very prestigious part of town. This man obviously was a person of influence and success, and it became very clear in his attitude how he felt about other folks. He was on a cell phone talking to one of his friends and responded to a comment made on the other end of the conversation by saying, "You're right. It's the way you and I think is the reason we make millions and the rest of them remain idiots!"

Regardless of the arrogance, it's tough to swallow when you realize your level of financial success has everything to do with your way of thinking and doing. The discussion that follows is not about making millions, however. It is about the importance of making million-dollar decisions today based on critical thinking and objective reality. These are the kind of decisions that determine a person's quality of life—a life without the burden of long-term, negative consequences. This refers specifically to certain types of debt (student loans and credit cards) that can have a painful and debilitating impact on your life tomorrow.

This raises the obvious question: How can parents and students avoid being seduced by foolish risks and misleading information about the value of a college education and the benefits of student loans? This choice should be based on a realistic decision-making model. A realistic model is one that helps you logically and rationally determine whether a four-year degree is really the smart way to achieve a satisfying, higher-paying job without debt. It is a model that reduces the irrationality of college selection and guides you to a school best suited to your career goals. That school is one that gives the best return on investment by preparing you to become a top earner at a reasonable cost (TERC).

This means using a questionnaire approach to determine whether to choose college or pursue a vocational/technical education. The right selection can determine your future success. The goal is to focus on prudent investing—cost versus projected value expected. It is, in my view, a better approach than accepting unrealistic costs (and loans) to obtain value hoped for, which means fulfilling personal wants rather than striving for the realistic needs of the job market.

The challenge for you is to balance the allure of a college education against the risk that you might not receive, obtain, or learn skills that are in high demand to insure financial success. Such calculations require time, knowledge, and effort on your part. Does this sound more like a business approach to you? The reality is the financial parts of life need to be treated like a business. The quality of your business decisions will determine your level of success.

Given the massive amounts of money at stake, does it not make sense to spend time and a few dollars up front, before investing or borrowing, to determine if a college education is the right way to go? There may be other options that align with your interests and skill set. The right decision is to make a good career choice, reduce risk, improve outcomes, and limit financial exposure. This will only make sense if a value-based education is a goal and a burning desire, not a fleeting dream.

Learn Your Lessons

See if your thinking and doing made the list in one or more of the following categories. If you read closely, there may even be a few lessons suggesting how to avoid educated poverty.

- Is your reason for going to college peer and parental pressure?

    Lesson: If so, a likely outcome will be obtaining a degree in an area of personal interest, which is easy but offers little value. When you borrow money to pursue a degree that is neither marketable nor in demand, you will not generate enough income to live a middle-class lifestyle. Change your approach and thinking if you are going to invest the money, time, and effort to go to college. Expect—no, *demand* of yourself—the maximization of that investment to generate future earnings necessary to lead a comfortable lifestyle while meeting all your obligations with ease.

- Could you be priority-challenged by waiting until graduation to discover that high-paying jobs in your degree field are not there? Remember, a lender requires payment without concern or sympathy for your situation or personal feelings. His attitude is, "Here's a quarter; call someone who cares!"

Lesson: It's up to you to avoid being forced into panic mode because you failed to plan for a good job and chose debt with its druglike addiction. Don't wait until your senior year to start job hunting; this places you at a disadvantage in the current job market. The best approach is to begin aggressively preparing for a post-college career during your time on campus. Forget about the college experience and concentrate on your future career by obtaining a marketable degree. You will have plenty of opportunity for the college experience; just don't make it your priority and focus.

To increase your chances of attaining not only meaningful but financially rewarding employment upon graduation, get started making contacts, gaining valuable work experience, creating a professional online presence, and building your résumé during your undergraduate years. By starting early, you begin to get a clearer idea of the kind of work you want to do, the type of work environment and opportunity desired, where best to use your skills, where to direct your interests, and how to secure a higher-paying job.

Be prepared for the workforce by continually building your résumé throughout college. Get acquainted with career services and resources offered on campus as early as possible. Make an appointment to get personalized advice and guidance early on and continue to do so as you advance in your degree program. Periodically revisit your goals and make sure you're still on track.

In addition to résumé and interview workshops, career centers can often put interested students in touch with alumni in their field of study. The more aware the centers are that you are seeking help and guidance and are putting in the effort as you prepare for future employment, the more likely they will connect you with alumni for informational interviews and relationship building.

This approach will enhance your value to a prospective employer, create a favorable impression, succinctly tell them how you can add value to their company, and allow them to ascertain your level of commitment. Gather market data, analyze it, and use it when engaging prospective employers. Interview the best experts available, gaining knowledge about the career you seek. Present a crystal-clear positive message that resonates with a prospective employer. Keep this in the forefront of your mission at all times: the world won't come to you, you have got to step out and step up if you have any chance of living the American dream.

- After spending time and somebody else's money earning a degree that leads to oblivion, will you become one of the 54 percent who have joined the ranks of more than 900,000 recent college graduates who either have no job or are underemployed?

Lesson: Don't get sucked in by ads from educational, governmental, and/or financial institutions to take on debt just so you can sign up for courses that lead nowhere. According to Course Hero reports, the US has more than 115,000 janitors, 16,000 parking-lot attendants, and 83,000 bartenders with degrees. That doesn't take into account those in food service, telemarketers, etc.

Now consider this: there are 3 million high-paying jobs going unfilled across the country, and many of those jobs may be in fields and/or locations you have no interest in whatsoever, until the you-know-what hits the fan. Why are so many graduates unwilling to look at skilled, hands-on jobs or positions, whether in manufacturing, various trades, oil fields, etc., where demand is high and the money is good? Is it a combination of false pride, an ill-chosen skill set, or lack of focus and/or motivation as to why they are not finding a higher-paying job?

If you want to be debt-free with a good income, get interested in a field/career that will provide it. Follow the money first. You can always indulge your personal interest later, after the basic needs of financial solvency have been met.

- Do you believe you are automatically entitled to achieve the American dream rather than earn it through self-reliance and a marketable degree?

Lesson: If so, I imagine Mom and Dad will be ecstatic when your dream job doesn't show up and you then ask to move back home.

- Do you feel you have allowed yourself to be led like a sheep down the path toward economic servitude or educated poverty via student loans?

  Lesson: If you have taken this route, now's the time to get real and get busy. Don't procrastinate or delay. Get a plan, work it, and begin filling up that hole you dug.

- Do you have the feeling that you don't know where you're going and used student loans to get there?

  Lesson: If that's the case, get on a different path quickly, or after four or five years of college, if you haven't dropped out, you will have acquired a nonessential or low-demand degree, which will not be enough to get a good-paying job to pay off those self-inflicted loans. Also, you will have failed to grasp the concept of payback by ignoring it until that lender comes a-calling demanding his due, ranging from $500 to $1,200 a month in combined private and federal loan payments.

- Did you spend a portion of your student loans on entertainment, toys (electronics), and frivolous items instead of applying it to the purpose intended?

  Lesson: Just remember: immediate gratification is short-lived, but debt misused can lead one into educated poverty.

- Do you qualify as an avoidance junkie? These are people who have allowed themselves to spend more time and money each month on a smartphone, social media gadgets and networks, gaming devices, and nonessential social activities, to the neglect of pursuing a highly marketable degree or going to the library to study. Many people waste valuable time and money (student loan funds?) to have the latest, greatest, and newest toy. The majority of these items will never be used to generate money to enhance your income, thereby becoming the biggest time- and money-wasters of your generation.

Lesson: Take a digital break. Analyze your actions and determine whether spending excessive amounts of time and money on these items is providing you with the educational and financial tools needed for a marketable degree. Periodically figure out how much time certain activities take by totaling up the minutes, hours, and cost involved. Consider, for instance, surfing the web, email, or texting. An hour a day equals 365 hours a year or fifteen days a year. Many students and adults are spending a lot more time than this with these items. Are you one of them?

Develop the habit of only checking your phone four or five times a day. It takes some practice to develop this habit, but it is life-changing. Rather than constantly checking, respond at designated times during the day; otherwise, you may wind up postponing important tasks, causing you to be stressed by last-minute deadlines. Don't fool yourself into thinking you are a multitasking wiz. Multitasking has been shown to be ineffective. Instead of trying to multitask, work at maximizing each task and prioritizing your time. Rather than trying to do two or more things at once, attack the highest priority of greatest importance that will generate the best return. It's usually the task with the greatest value, as it can serve several connected purposes.

- Do you believe working while going to college keeps you from having the total college experience, such as extracurricular activities that include campus organizations, fraternities, sororities, and partying? Do you also feel developing social skills and contacts are more important than dealing with money issues and career-enhancement studies?

  Lesson: A prospective employer will want to know how you used your time and maximized your efforts in developing job skills and discipline that will add value to their company or organization.

You can't afford to wait until your junior or senior year to get serious about securing a well-paying job when you graduate. Realistically, you must start the process with action and a plan during your senior year in high school, which will lead you to your desired results at college graduation. It's always about marketing, image, and having the right skill set an employer needs. That's what you must focus on.

Consider seeking an internship, as it can help you develop an understanding of what the workplace is really like. It can be an eye-opener, skill-enhancer, and life-changer. The experience stands out on a résumé, as many employers today prefer prospective hires who have internship experience on their profile. The reasoning is that a graduate who has worked as an intern will more readily adapt to a business culture, reduce training time, and become more productive more quickly.

However, any kind of work-related experience can be just as valuable. This would include campus jobs, such as working in the library or an office where valuable customer-service skills can be learned. Campus maintenance, construction crews, and fast-food services provide great experience working in team situations, all of which teaches one how to be timely as well as develop professionalism in a working environment.

- Do you consider yourself to be financially astute? Or are you one of the 70 percent of college graduates who have accumulated in excess of $35,000 in student loans and credit card debt not knowing what the effect of compounding interest upon interest has, and will have, on your future ability to pay off your loans?

  Lesson: When evaluating student loan balances versus projected employment income, keep the 35 percent rule of thumb in front in mind at all times. As an example, if you borrow $25,000, you will need a job paying 35 percent more per year than the total principal of your loans, or $37,500, in order to meet future obligations without stress. If you borrow $70,000, you will need a job paying $94,500. Not many of those out there.

Are you on the way to becoming a debt addict? This could be the case if you think student loans and credit card debt are to be used indiscriminately at your whim while repayments are not worth worrying about, as your parents are doing okay and seem to be managing their debt without any problems. Do you believe you won't have to make responsible decisions for your financial life until after graduation? In your thinking and doing, are you demonstrating an attitude that, although you want relief from your loan obligations, you aren't willing to pay the price, make the sacrifice, or do the homework to pay a self-inflicted debt off?

Lesson: It's time to get back on track and embrace a mind-set that comes down to focusing on just two or three priorities at a time—those that will get you to where you want to go. Turn off the noise around you and focus on these key things. Say no to the many distractions tempting you. This is a key trait possessed by the most successful leaders and doers, so why not follow their lead?

- Do you think your parents and society owe you a college education?

    Lesson: Parents owe you encouragement and guidance, yes. However, a student needs to assume ownership, as it's your future life and career that's at stake. Students must take on responsibility by aggressively seeking the most beneficial, cost-effective ways, academically and financially, to attain a degree or trade. You have to get mentally tough, become a proactive activist, and focus on creating the kind of healthy financial future the America dream is based on.

- Are you going to allow your parents to go broke supporting you, your debt obligations, and your lifestyle by jeopardizing their retirement savings, lifestyle, and medical care?

    Lesson: Symptoms of this affliction are selfishness and shiftlessness along with various degrees of disrespectfulness. If you choose to continue on this path, by the time you're thirty years old, your parents will still be giving excuses for your failure to take responsibility for your life in a mature manner, telling folks you are still searching for yourself. Before you realize it, you will be forty—and if you choose to continue with the same lifestyle and behavior patterns, your parents will avoid the issue of your failing to contribute to society altogether, because to do so they would have to include the term *bum* in their answer.

- Have you willingly and literally taken the loan way out? If so, was it because it was easy to borrow tens of thousands of dollars to attend college without accountability? And now that it's payback time, do you want a bailout and forgiveness for choosing to be gullible and an easy sell?

  Lesson: Unfortunately, under today's legal obligations, you are between a rock and a hard place. You must find ways to honor your debt, and if that means taking on two extra jobs and making the sacrifices, then get it done. If your goal is to be a contender in life and not an observer or bystander, then pull yourself up and do whatever it takes by becoming a doer.

- Do you fail to grasp the concept that it's nobody's fault but your own that you can't buy a nice house or a decent car after graduation because you have to repay student loan debt?

  Lesson: Before you splurge by taking on student loans, think very carefully, understand fully what's required, and realize how that loan balance can explode exponentially in the future, derailing your American dream with unintended consequences. If you take it on, just remember, it was your decision to do so. It will be yours to own, possibly forever. Remember, laws make it so lenders can come after your estate.

Call to Action

Some 65 percent of college graduates say the American dream is dead. Don't be one of them. The American dream is not a handout or entitlement, and the best way to achieve it is to embrace the following steps outlined by

Robert Collier in *The Secret of the Ages*. His master formula of attainment is as follows. You may have anything you want, provided you

- know exactly what you want,
- want it hard enough,
- confidently expect to attain it,
- persistently determine to obtain it, and
- are willing to pay the price of its attainment.

Rise to summa cum laude status while pursuing the American dream by embracing the master formula of attainment as you commit and follow through on these top 10 reasons to graduate college debt-free:

1. I must effectively handle my own money issues; otherwise, how can I expect a company to hire me into a position of fiscal responsibility?
2. I refuse to be a burden on my parents and society, so I will honor them and my country by being self-reliant.
3. I will increase my chances of becoming a millionaire 1,000 percent by graduating debt-free.
4. I will not be paying off student loans when Britney Spears has grandkids.
5. I will not have to dig myself out of a long-term financial hole.
6. I will not have to worry how I'm going to live from one paycheck to another.
7. I will not have to sell my golf clubs, iPads, CDs, TVs, etc. on eBay.
8. I plan on having money in the bank and being in demand socially.
9. My financial health is more important than the stress and depression of debt suffocation.
10. My goal is to achieve an in-demand, marketable degree debt-free, thereby demonstrating that I have a responsible grip on reality, both financially and academically.

The Bottom Line

Don't count on the government to provide financial solutions, as they are expensive. Go out and create your own solutions through individual action. Make your own choices based on facts, not emotions. Do your homework, research, and network. Whether you're a high school student thinking about college or a parent fretting about the obscene costs of a college education, think outside the box and begin planning in earnest the necessary steps.

Make no mistake about it: a strong work ethic focused on achieving high grades and working full-time (summers) and part-time (school year) is extremely important and an early predictor of success. Without the commitment, willingness, and hard work required in the pursuit of your goal, scholarships will be tougher to come by, and so will that high-paying job you seek after graduation. Remember, based on your attitude and actions, history tends to repeat itself. Sometimes, so does stupid.

If you want to find out why you are getting the outcomes and results you are in life related to money and debt, do a thorough examination of your beliefs that brought you to this state of existence. Beliefs are the cause (your thinking and doing) leading you to the effect (your outcomes and results). When you upgrade or change your behavior, you upgrade and change your results. If you believe you're a champion, then train like a champion. If you believe there is no light at the end of the tunnel, a loser's fate becomes your reward.

The How

The way to debt-free success is not for the lazy or unmotivated. It's not going to be easy. It's not for those who should have never gone to college in the first place. You must develop a mind-set as outlined in *The Master Formula of Attainment* to do whatever it takes.

People who succeed in life work hard at succeeding. It doesn't necessarily happen because they are blessed with talent or just lucky. The reality is that most of them work harder and smarter than the average person. That is why they are winners. They are not willing to settle for mediocrity or just maintaining the status quo.

Whether top athletes, business owners, or outstanding executives, these people are known for waking up early, working toward a goal while others are still in bed, and staying at the task later than everyone else. They work six or seven days a week, sixty-five to eighty hours. Can anyone do it? Yes, anyone who is 100 percent focused on a goal, willing to engage in old-fashioned hard work (mentally and physically), not easily swayed or distracted, and in the game of life for the long term.

You begin by treating your situation as a business. You must create a marketing and action plan, then apply old-fashioned hard work. This will not be a short-term or instant gratification goal, and it makes sense to do your research up front on selecting and preparing for a well-paying career. Why invest time chasing a low-paying job when there are so many higher-paying careers out there?

If you have taken on a student loan, find out where you can attain employment that will allow you to pay off that loan quickly. Remember, the goal is to get the loan reduced, forgiven, or paid off, and there are various enterprises and communities out there that can help you do that. However, you must seek them out and be willing to make sacrifices as well as go into a field that may not align with your degree.

Pare your living, socializing, and entertainment expenses down to a bare minimum. Use the extra money to pay off your debt and build a savings reserve. By sacrificing now, you will be building a solid foundation that will position you to achieve your long-term goals at a later date.

If you have put forth maximum effort to secure a job in your career field without success before graduation, then only allow thirty days after graduation to find that job. Devote at least fifty hours per week toward that end. At the end of thirty days, most people would be running out of money, so now it is important to get temporary employment. Remember, do whatever it takes.

Work two jobs if necessary, six or seven days a week, to make it happen. Become an effective networker during these times to help you land better-paying employment. Be open-minded. Learn as much from each job as possible, make the best of each experience, and use those newly acquired skills to help you find and/or create a better-paying situation. Don't overlook entrepreneurial activities.

The Right Dream

Some people waste their lives following dreams they'll never achieve. Pursuing the right dream is critical—not the dream with immediate gratification or the one coupled with excessive financial cost. It's the one with long-term benefits, serving a specific purpose and meeting a need.

We've been told that "all it takes is a dream, and you can accomplish whatever your heart desires." This philosophy is espoused by motivational gurus, various experts, teachers, and preachers. However, it must be the right dream, or you will spend years chasing a delusion. How can you avoid that?

First and foremost, you have to do the time. It's a question of commitment. What foundation are you laying today for success tomorrow? What classes are you taking, and what kind of grades are you making? What kind of part-time work are you doing? Have you found a mentor or coach? Are you searching for any and all scholarships and grants?

How many students could have avoided years of disappointment and debt if only someone would have told them the truth? There comes a time to stop following just any dream and spend more time discovering the right dream to follow. A great life doesn't happen by accident, luck, or wishful thinking. It happens by being clear on exactly what you want out of life, preparing for that outcome (by acquiring skills and knowledge), and applying the right thinking and doing combined with action, commitment, persistence, and willingness to make sacrifices.

Unless you are willing to make a commitment to achieve that dream you seek, you're simply wasting your life. How can you avoid spending years pursuing a delusion? The key is discovering the right dream. Remember the memorable scene in the movie *City Slickers*?

> Curly: Do you know what the secret of life is? [Holds up one finger] This!
> Mitch: Your finger?
> Curly: One thing. Just one thing. You stick to that and the rest don't mean s***.
> Mitch: But what is the "one thing?"
> Curly: That's what you have to find out.

Stand Up

There can be no higher calling than for you to honor, respect, and protect your parents from actions and responsibilities resulting from bad choices and decisions on your part related to student loans and credit card debt. As a student, you need to understand that your parents do not owe you a college education. A student needs to assume ownership, and one way is to aggressively seek the most cost-effective means, academically and financially, to attain that degree or trade.

Your parents protected you while you were growing up. They supported you along the way with housing, food, clothing, entertainment, and encouragement. They financed your education. They made sacrifices.

Now it's your turn to make them proud by fulfilling their dreams and expectations for you by giving your best effort to obtain a well-paying, satisfying career; making wise financial decisions based on logic and critical thinking; striving for a successful life outside the home; and above all, not allowing your parents to go broke supporting you and your lifestyle.

> *America has a way of making the impossible seem inevitable, but we know it was never inevitable. It took leadership. And it took courage.* — Condoleezza Rice

Student Loans as a Financial Tool

Student loans are a tool—an emergency fund—not a sack of money to blow on personal gratification. Parents and students must acknowledge and embrace this fact. Life is a business, and how well you manage your business determines the outcomes and results in your life. Student loans are only one tool to help finance the development of a marketable and in-demand product, which is you, the future graduate. However, student loans have a greater cost (financial and emotional) associated with them and consequently should be used only in conjunction with strategic planning, resolve, and commitment.

Caveat emptor—"let the buyer beware"—is the contract-law principle that controls the sale not only of property after the date of closing but also the sale of other goods. The phrase and its use as a disclaimer of warranties arises from the fact that buyers typically have less information about what they are purchasing, while the seller has more information. The quality of this situation is known as *information asymmetry*. Defects in the goods or services may be hidden from the buyer and only known to the seller.

When it comes to student loans, make sure the phrase "let the buyer beware" is embedded in your mind and not forgotten or avoided. It is important to know and understand exactly what you're signing. The best surprise is no surprise at all. Student loans often are the first legal obligation young people enter into. Make sure you do your homework on this, including checking out what the monthly payments will be over the next ten years after repayment begins.

Also research the most cost-effective schools that give the greatest return on investment (career enhancement) and develop a financial plan to achieve your goals. After these are completed, it's time to apply an objective analysis of the results. If the outcome of those results conclusively determines that student loans are necessary to reach your objective, then I recommend the following:

- Read all paperwork thoroughly and understand the responsibility, obligations, and requirements of those loans, whether private or government. If you choose to proceed, then make them work for you.
- Set aside 25 percent of the money borrowed as an emergency fund as well as a cushion to have available in repaying the debt after graduation.
- Use 25 percent of the borrowed funds as an investment into a profit-generating opportunity, either work-related or a sideline business.
- Use the remaining 50 percent exclusively for tuition, books, and direct school-related expenses.
- Provide the balance of the cost by working full-time between semesters and part-time during school. Save, save, save while earning and paying your own way.
- Finally, pursue scholarships and grants with tenacity and persistence. These do not require payback but only require you to honor the conditions upon which they were granted.

All that a man achieves and all that he fails to achieve is the direct result of his own thoughts. — James Allen

Get Serious about Financing Your Education

Unlimited partying, costly spring break excursions, and uncontrolled spending does not define a future graduate as a marketable product deserving of a high-paying career. Either you get tough and actively pursue your American dream, or you may find yourself headed down into an abyss of self-pity, unproductivity, and dead-end jobs.

You are in one of the biggest games of your life: learning, practicing, and preparing for the transition into adulthood, where you take on and effectively deal with the realities of life. Whether you win or lose depends on your commitment, resolve, and perseverance, so commit and get it done.

The way to wealth, if you desire it, is as plain as the way to the market. It depends chiefly on two words, industry and frugality; that is waste neither time nor money, but make the best use of both. — Benjamin Franklin

If you are considering student loans without a specific strategic plan, you could very possibly be gambling away your future. It should be excruciatingly clear that in gambling, the odds always favor the house, or in this case, the lender. Students and parents both need to understand, to the core of their being, the long-term risk associated with student loans.

Be informed, be aware, and be extremely cautious when considering this avenue to finance a college education. There are always options. However, it takes courage, effort, and persistence to pursue these, as they are not for the lazy and entitlement-minded, or for those expecting a free ride without sacrifice.

To explore what some of these might be, continue reading. That will pay big dividends when you make the decision to get serious in your approach to financing a college education. The approach to succeed begins with the right mind-set, taking a realistic view of the process, and developing a doable plan which will allow you to achieve your goal of living the American dream.

If your heartfelt desire is to live the American dream, then all those around you must do their part by doing the necessary homework and making the effort and sacrifices necessary to achieve that goal. This dream is almost impossible to reach without a committed, full-fledged effort. The alternative—using student loans—carries with it the possibility of being buried with suffocating student debt and living in educated poverty.

If you want to keep student loans from threatening your American dream, understand fully what you are getting into when you take on student debt. I challenge you to share and embrace the information in this book and put into play its lessons, thereby saving you and your loved ones the heartache of living with suffocating debt tomorrow.

Chapter 6
Educators

Don't be so focused on testing results that you ignore the challenges facing your students when they have to confront life's realities. Education must be balanced. It must recognize the needs of industry as well as students for skills on how to survive and prosper within today's society. If schools are allowed to put students at risk with debt for the rest of their working lives by failing to include in the curriculum principles and practices of financial education, an unfathomable number will graduate with degrees in educated poverty.

According to the US Department of Education, less than 50 percent of those starting college fail to graduate, and it seems those students' main accomplishment is successfully acquiring debt without a degree and securing a low-paying job. Most parents want to hear how their students are doing and all about their accomplishments. The result? Many students are coming home as flag-bearers symbolizing the failure of our educational system, its educators, and society.

Overwhelming student loan debt in the pursuit of a college degree is not a precursor to success. It is, however, an indicator of failure on the part of parents, the educational system, and students themselves. If the pupil hasn't learned, the teacher hasn't taught.

Stepping Up to the Plate

One way educators can help parents and students track progress is by teaching and utilizing a variation of a critical path method program. CPM is a step-by-step technique (road map) for process planning that defines critical and noncritical tasks with the goal of preventing time-frame problems and process bottlenecks. In other words, it's about keeping the train on the tracks and on schedule.

CPM was developed in the 1950s by DuPont and was first used in missile-defense construction projects. Since then, CPM has been adapted to other fields, including hardware and software product research and development. CPM is ideally suited to projects consisting of numerous activities that interact in a complex manner. In many ways, a pathway to a college degree fits within this type of framework.

A modified CPM model, or a comparable process, should be put in play in education. This identifies and charts the definitive steps and tasks involved along with planned actions necessary to achieve the end result—in this case, a college degree and a rewarding career for the motivated student. A few of the most important items are briefly summarized as follows:

- Define the required tasks and put them down in an ordered (sequenced) list.
- Create a flowchart or other diagram showing each task in relation to the others.
- Identify the critical and noncritical relationships (paths) among tasks allowing for variables.
- Determine the expected completion or execution time for each task.
- Locate or devise alternatives (backups) for the most critical paths and unexpected events.
- Project a final completion date.

Call to Action

I believe high schools, colleges, and universities should create an award for teachers who effectively advocate for and instruct students on how to effectively manage their finances. Criteria could include the following:

- Provide and incorporate realistic financial teaching models at the K-12 levels and college.

- Teach students the financial realities of life before, during, and after college.
- Teach self-reliant strategies that will help students achieve a college education and success in life.
- Advocate as well as model effective money practices and behaviors using the best resources available.
- Enlist methods and processes to help students develop critical thinking skills to better evaluate options and choices available.
- Use financial models to determine the true cost of college along with the value and benefits of financial education.
- Plan ways to achieve the investment needed for college by avoiding unnecessary student loan and credit card debt.

And why is this important? Because money mismanagement—as reported by a substantial number of veterans, college graduates, and dropouts—was related to a higher rate of subsequent homelessness. The findings have implications for policymakers and clinicians, suggesting that financial education in the early years would be extremely beneficial in reducing homelessness among these people.

Chapter 7
Bankers and Lenders Role

> *A feeble man can see the farms that are fenced and tilled, the houses that are built. The strong man sees the possible houses and farms. His eye makes estates as fast as the sun breeds clouds.*
> — *Ralph Waldo Emerson*

This is an area of opportunity for committed, responsible, and forward-thinking financial institutions—such as banks and savings and loans—to step up into a service role of providing sound and realistic coaching in financial management, stability, and growth. Their interest should be focused on developing long-term solid financial customers and not primarily generating immediate fees and placing burdensome debt on unaware and poorly informed students and parents.

Don't misunderstand me on this point. It's not the bank's responsibility to take over or take on financial education. However, they just may be in the best position to supplement and shore up what's lacking in the teaching of sound financial practices in our families and educational programs. They could do so by offering exciting, challenging, and rewarding seminars and workshops, or even sponsoring summer camps on financial management and planning. It would be important to add certain how-to programs to assist in helping participants develop the mentality and discipline to achieve financial freedom.

Successful individuals and business leaders could be brought into the programs to teach the financial practices and strategies they employ. These practices and strategies would be no-nonsense, practical, and hands-on. If used every day, they would lead participants to financial independence. Their teachings would be backed up with the principles and values necessary for personal and financial growth. Essential coursework could include checkbook use; credit and debit card management; budgeting; conservative saving and investing practices; income and debt management; and the techniques for building a sizable bank account. There would be no selling or promoting of speculative or risky products designed to drain the pocketbook and the bank accounts of the participants.

Sponsoring financial institutions could also set up a results-based incentive and/or a scholarship program for successful graduates. The possibilities to make a difference in helping to develop financially responsible young adults begins by taking the first step to make it happen. An aware and knowledgeable student today is a long-term stream of solid business for the bank tomorrow.

The following are considered important, definite, and common-sense rules to live by in certain professions and should be combined into a clear and specific code of conduct applying to lenders, specifically those issuing student loans:

- *Fiduciary rule*—The Department of Labor's fiduciary rule requires financial professionals who give advice about retirement accounts to put their clients' interests ahead of their own. Advisors are not to conceal any potential conflict of interest, and all fees and commissions for retirement plans and retirement planning advice must be clearly disclosed in dollar form to clients.
- *Hippocratic oath*—In the medical profession, another equivalent phrase is found in *Epidemics, Book I*. The Hippocratic oath states: "First, Do No Harm. Practice two things in your dealings with disease: Either help or do not harm the patient."

Charley's Code of Conduct for Lenders

The borrower is granted the same status as a client, thereby establishing a fiduciary relationship involving trust, transparency, and full disclosure without fear or risk of being led or placed in an untenable position based on hidden and undisclosed information that may not be in the client's best interest, now or in the future. The lender is required to carefully, completely, and with integrity represent the client's best interest.

Chapter 8
Politicians

Before proceeding, I recommend you go back to Chapter 1: The Good, The Bad, and The Ugly, and review the promises, laws, and regulations that have created another financial bubble: a $1.5 trillion dollar house of cards causing irreparable harm to financially challenged parents, students, and the nation as a whole. Proof of the impact and negative consequences of legislation passed is irrefutable. It must be changed to bring about fairness as well as redesigned to refocus the emphasis on self-reliance—the American way—and not the short-term gratification of the loan way to achieve the American dream.

It's evident, or should be at this point, that financial education is severely lacking in our homes and our educational and governmental institutions. Because of this gross oversight and neglect, many individuals have not developed practical, working, and street-smart knowledge of personal finance, making them easy prey for lenders with questionable agendas. Naive parents, students, and politicians tend to be overly influenced by the "experts" in the financial-aid area who are offering what appears to be an easy way to afford a college education.

As Congress and various politicians have dithered, danced, and sidestepped the real issue by diverting attention to quick fixes and handing out pacifiers, they have done nothing substantive about the real problem. Until lawmakers get busy on practical, realistic solutions, it's only going to get worse.

Perhaps the real truth lies here: the cash cow. The Government Accountability Office reports that the federal government is projected to earn $50 billion from student loans this year. It is estimated the government will pocket an additional $185 billion in profits on new student loans made during the next ten years or $18.5 billion per year.

This raises the question: Is the government in the student loan business altruistically or exploitatively? If altruistically, how much reasonable profit is acceptable over and above its costs? If it is exploitatively, and from all indications it is, is this an appropriate and defensible role of government? Who really benefits financially? It's not the 70 percent of graduates with debt to repay. It's the lenders, educational institutions, and federal government.

Lenders are not concerned about the financial health of the borrower, so it should be our representatives who are looking out for the best interest of their constituency and the health of our country. That means full disclosure and transparency must be made upfront, noting who the real beneficiaries are. Instead, we get spin, saying it's to students' advantage to borrow their way through college. "Bankers and lenders encourage people to borrow beyond their means, preying especially on those who are financially unsophisticated," said Joseph Stiglitz, Nobel Memorial Prize winner in economics and former chairman of the Council of Economic Advisers. As a result, student loan defaults are skyrocketing.

Review Charley's Code of Conduct for Lenders, which states, "The borrower is granted the same status as a client, thereby establishing a fiduciary relationship involving trust, transparency, and full disclosure without fear or risk of being led or placed in an untenable position based on hidden and undisclosed information that may not be in the client's best interest, now or in the future. The lender is required to carefully, completely and with integrity represent the client's best interest."

Compare that to Stiglitz's stark description: "Student debt has become an integral part of the story of American inequality ... We now have a pay-to-play, winner-take-all game where the wealthiest are assured a spot, and the rest are compelled to take a gamble on huge debts, with no guarantee of a payoff."

Students in the past somehow managed to pay their debt without the government jumping in to rescue them, even though they were paying a far higher interest rate. It appears now that the mind-set of entitlement is the model subtly pushed onto yet another group of Americans, which is troubling on so many levels. The perception is that Washington and Wall

Street have us utterly convinced the only answer to fighting back against economic injustice is to hand over even more power to the very systems that got us into this pickle in the first place.

Nowhere is this more evident than the current hubbub over student loans. While certainly understandable, the "Where's my bailout?" mentality of some of the student loan activists is incredibly destructive, because the system (Wall Street and Washington) will be only too happy to oblige with a solution—one that makes the student borrower worse off while making the lenders even wealthier and more powerful, unfortunately with the blessing of our legislators.

If the government didn't guarantee student loans, most students wouldn't have a loan to begin with, nor would they need one, because college would be more affordable. Guaranteed student loans don't necessarily mean greater access to education. What they do mean is higher education costs and a huge profit center for financial, educational, and governmental institutions.

The student loan system (private and governmental) is not designed to provide better education opportunities for the young but rather to indenture them in an atrocious form of lifelong debt servitude to financial institutions and the federal government. In addition, it is one of the key factors contributing to the decline of the middle class.

Teachable Moments

Does your personal thinking and doing make the following list? Check all that apply:

- ☐ Do you believe that students actually benefit educationally, financially, and career-wise in the long term by borrowing their way through college?

    Lesson: Guaranteed student loans don't necessarily mean greater access to education. What they do mean is higher education costs and a huge profit center for financial, educational, and governmental institutions. Lenders, and it seems most politicians, are not concerned about the financial health of the borrower (their current or future constituent) when there's a government guarantee coming in the back door. In reality, the lender is indenturing the student into lifelong economic slavery. Whatever happened to the concept of responsible lending and borrowing?

- ☐ Do you buy into the argument that these laws, regulations, and strategies are necessary because student borrowers who default are robbing the taxpayers?

  Lesson: The truth is, guarantors and collection companies make a tremendous amount of profit when these loans go into default. In addition, the federal government benefits by receiving $1.20 for every dollar paid out in default claims.

- ☐ When it comes to student loan legislation, do major financial institutions, lenders, and their representatives provide specific information, guidelines, and drafts of recommended solutions (laws, rules, and regulations) that favor (protect) the lender over the borrower?

  Lesson: If so, then it is apparent, but not transparent, that the unintended (or intended) consequences have led to another financial bubble—a $1.5 trillion dollar house of cards causing irreparable harm to students and our nation as a whole. Is it any wonder 67 percent of college graduates think the American dream is dead?

Call to Action

Become a summa cum laude candidate for responsible representation by standing tall on the following:

- Be the first line of defense and safeguard the freedoms necessary to pursue the American dream as granted by the Declaration of Independence, the Constitution, and the Bill of Rights.

- Determine what actions need to be taken to keep parents and students out of harm's way when it comes to the long-term financial consequences of guaranteed government programs.
- Advocate full disclosure (truth and consequences) transparency by revealing who really benefits financially from student loans.
- Discredit the spin and BS of those advocates who say it's to students' advantage to borrow their way through college.
- Correct past legislation and regulations that weaken the soul of self-reliance, thereby manifesting an entitlement mentality.
- Restrict government's role in doing what parents and students should be doing for themselves.
- Prevent funding actions (bailouts) on the part of the government toward troubled sectors in our industry, such as banks and energy and automobile companies. Provide and allow the same bankruptcy protection to student loan borrowers as granted to corporations that have been granted person status; otherwise, students will be justified in chanting their rallying cry, "Where's my bailout?"
- Get the government out of the guaranteed student loan business. As the American dream is not guaranteed for the borrower, it should not be guaranteed for the lender.
- Most importantly, level the playing field by repealing those sections of the Bankruptcy Reform Act of 1978 and especially the 1998 Amendments to the Higher Education Act and the 2005 Bankruptcy Abuse Prevention and Consumer Protection Act that unjustly, discriminatingly, and prejudicially single out and remove bankruptcy and default protections from student loan borrowers, cosigners, and consumers.
- Finally, do the right thing. Protect our student citizens from predatory lending practices by preparing them through required financial education beginning in the K-12 levels along with the principals of common sense, fairness, and equal justice for all.

First, do no harm!

Afterword

You need to be highly motivated and do the homework before your kids reach college age. If your children are heading to college, both you and your students need to be extremely cautious, knowledgeable, and fully aware of the long-term consequences of student loans. You must do the research as well as understand the future commitment, consequences, and possible ramifications of your decisions.

I believe there is still hope for change in how students, parents, educators, and politicians deal with these issues by adopting realistic methods and strategies for determining the best career choices to make, requiring the least amount of money and yielding the greatest return for the effort. If people continue to choose the ways advocated by the government, financial, and educational institutions, many will wind up in a long-term debt suffocation situation.

Unfortunately, ways of paying for higher education have changed, as parents and students rely on loans as a matter of course. This has created a mind-set (delusional thinking) driving the average parent and student to find easy, less courageous ways of getting a college degree. Subconsciously and unfortunately, those students and parents are projecting a mentality that student loans are the lazy man's way to a college education.

It is interesting to note that this is one of the key factors involved in a major philosophical shift toward debt in recent years among today's families compared to earlier generations. The long-range effects of student loans and credit card debt are now adding another crucial factor to the financial strain on the diminishing middle class in America.

The compounding consequence of higher-paying jobs being shipped overseas together with the crippling effect of student loans has created the underemployed crisis in this country. Our middle class is going the way of the Hindenburg. It is a disaster in the making.

The importance of teaching our children the value, benefit, and rewards of a solid financial education cannot be understated. It requires commitment, persistence, effort, and sacrifice to achieve the goal—the essential ingredients necessary for success in life. It must be kept in mind that our college graduates are future parents as well as future leaders of our communities, states, and country.

Using the best resources available, parents and educators must advocate the teaching of, as well as modeling in words and deeds, effective financial practices and behaviors. Only then will students be prepared to deal with the financial realities of life before, during, and after college. If this area of learning is neglected, the consequences become a burden for all. It turns into a lifetime of debt for parents and students who wind up with an albatross anchored to their backs and a life full of educated poverty.

Don't let this be you, or my next book will be *It's the Parents, Educators, and Politicians, Stupid!*

About the Author

Charley's journey has taken him from the eastern farm hills of Kansas to military service, college administration, and the real estate industry. He has degrees in business and education plus an extensive background in management. His career as a professional entertainer and author began later in life.

What he shares—in an inspirational, humorous, or informational way—is a direct reflection of his life experiences. Many of his stories are of various people he's met along the way, some who inspired him, some who opened doors, and a few who tried to discourage him. He also tells of life events that challenged the depth of his faith and situations that gave him hope, inspiration, and courage to follow his dream.

His research on student debt has given him a unique insight into the social and economic impact of this oftentimes overwhelming albatross. His books are directed toward parents with a focus on college cost, impact of long-term student loan debt, and career choices. He believes it's important for parents to work with their children in developing self-reliant plans to minimize dependence upon student loans while focusing on the right college degree and financial freedom.

One of his books, *Debt-Free College Education or a Debtor's Burden?*, challenges the way parents, students, and educators approach a college education. Charley's goal is to encourage them to choose the path of opportunity and financial literacy versus one of student loans, credit card debt, and debt suffocation. The Debt-Free College Education series is designed to assist and guide parents as well as educators in helping future collegians develop self-reliant attitudes in their career pursuits along with realistic financial plans.

Charley's presentations are informative and timely. They challenge the way parents, students, and educators approach a college education. Contact Charley at charleygreen@charleygreen.com for interviews or to schedule a presentations to your group or organization. You can also find him on Facebook as Charley Green, Author.

The Debt-Free College Education Series is designed to assist and guide parents as well as educators in helping future collegians develop self-reliant attitudes in their career pursuits along with realistic financial plans.

Other books available at www.CharleyGreen.com:

How to Keep Student Loans From Threatening Your American Dream

Debt-Free College Education or A Debtor's Burden?

The Reluctant Warrior: The Journey Begins

Will Rogers and Charley

Pamphlet: "Seven Things You Must Know About Student Loans: The Good, The Bad, and The Ugly"

Ways to use this book:

Give it as a gift to parents of college-bound students.

Give copies to schools, educational groups, and organizations to use as handouts to members, faculty, or students.

Send as a thank-you to your customers for their business.

Mail a book to your prospect list to stay in touch with them.

Use it as a Christmas card; the cover can be overprinted.

Give it away at PTA and educational meetings or conferences to help bring attention to this issue.

Give it as an incentive for completing a survey form.

Include it as a thank-you for an order when sending an invoice or statement.

Bundle or package several books as a value-added bonus for ordering a particular product.

Use as prizes in a raffle or charity event.

Use a book to launch a new product, including product details in the center of the book.